T0344461

6G and Next-Generation Internet

The sixth generation (6G) of wireless cellular networks is expected to incorporate the latest developments in network infrastructure and emerging advances in technology. It will not only explore more spectrum at high-frequency bands but also converge driving technological trends, including connected robotics, artificial intelligence (AI), and blockchain technologies. There is also a strong notion that the nature of mobile terminals will change, whereby intelligent mobile robots are anticipated to play a more important role. Importantly, 6G will become more human-centered than 5G, which primarily focused on industry verticals.

This book explores the human-centeredness of blockchain and Web3 economy for the 6G era. Aimed at graduate students, network and blockchain researchers, professionals, engineers, and practitioners, this book discusses the symbiosis of blockchain with other key technologies such as AI and robots, while putting the focus on the Tactile Internet for advanced human-to-machine interaction. By focusing on the research field of robonomics in the 6G Era, which studies the social integration of robots into the economy and human society, the book puts the various developed ideas and concepts into the perspective of the future Super Smart Society 5.0.

Abdeljalil Beniiche received his PhD in telecommunications from the Institut National de la Recherche Scientifique (INRS), Montréal, Canada. His research focuses on 6G networks, Tactile Internet, blockchain, information security, behavioral economics, and Society 5.0. His research findings have been published in many prestigious journals, such as *IEEE Network, IEEE Wireless Communications, IEEE Communications Magazine*, and *IEEE/OSA Journal of Optical Communications and Networking*. He has served and continues to serve on the technical program committees and a reviewer of numerous major international conferences, journals, and magazines. Currently, he is a Security Architect in the financial industry.

6G and Next-Generation Internet
Under Blockchain Web3 Economy

Abdeljalil Beniiche

CRC Press
Taylor & Francis Group
Boca Raton London New York

CRC Press is an imprint of the
Taylor & Francis Group, an **informa** business

First edition published 2024
by CRC Press
2385 Executive Center Drive, Suite 320, Boca Raton, FL 33431

and by CRC Press
4 Park Square, Milton Park, Abingdon, Oxon, OX14 4RN

CRC Press is an imprint of Taylor & Francis Group, LLC

© 2024 Abdeljalil Beniiche

ISBN: 978-1-032-54241-6 (hbk)
ISBN: 978-1-032-54744-2 (pbk)
ISBN: 978-1-003-42732-2 (ebk)

DOI: 10.1201/9781003427322

Typeset in Times
by KnowledgeWorks Global Ltd.

Contents

Acknowledgment   ix
List of Acronyms   xi

1 6G-Blockchain: Vision and Research Directions   1
Background and Motivation   1
      Evolution of Mobile Networks and Internet   1
      6G Vision   5
      Blockchain and Distributed Ledger Technologies   8
Advanced Blockchain Technologies: Prior Art and
Recent Progress   11
      DAO   11
      Blockchain Oracles   13
      Token Engineering   15
From Industry 4.0 toward Society 5.0   16
      Cyber-Physical-Social Systems (CPSS)   16
      Industry 5.0   17
      Society 5.0   18
Purpose and Outline of Book   19
Notes   21
References   21

**2 Blockchain, AI, and Human Intelligence: The Path
toward 6G   25**
Introduction   25
Blockchain Technologies   27
      Ethereum versus Bitcoin Blockchains   28
      Decentralized Autonomous Organizations (DAOs)   31
Blockchain IoT and Edge Computing   33
      Blockchain IoT (B-IoT): Recent Progress and Related Work   33
      Blockchain-Enabled Edge Computing   36
The IEEE P1918.1 Tactile Internet   38
      The Tactile Internet: Key Principles   38
      Human-Agent-Robot Teamwork   40

Low-Latency FiWi-Enhanced LTE-A HetNets with
AI-Enhanced MEC   41
Decentralizing the Tactile Internet   44
Decentralized Edge Intelligence   45
Crowdsourcing: Expanding the HO Workforce   47
Blockchain, AI, and Human Intelligence: The Path Forward   48
Cognitive-Assistance-Based Intelligence Amplification   48
HITL Hybrid-Augmented Intelligence   48
The Rise of the Decentralized Self-Organizing Cooperative 49
Nudging toward Human Augmentation   49
Open Challenges and Future Work   50
Conclusions   50
Note   51
References   51

3 **DAO-Based Trusted Collaboration and Social Cohesion
Approach for the 6G-Tactile Internet**   **54**
Introduction   54
Decentralizing the Tactile Internet   56
FiWi Enhanced Mobile Networks: Spreading Ownership   56
AI-Enhanced MEC   58
Crowdsourcing   60
Nudging: From Judge Contract to Nudge Contract   62
Cognitive Assistance: From AI to Intelligence
Amplification (IA)   62
HITL Hybrid-Augmented Intelligence   63
Decentralized Self-Organizing Cooperative (DSOC)   63
Nudge Contract: Nudging via Smart Contract   64
Results   64
Conclusions   66
Notes   66
References   67

4 **Blockchain Meets 6G: Social Human-Robot Interaction
through Oracles and Behavioral Economics**   **68**
Introduction   68
6G Vision: Blockchains and Robots   70
Blockchain Benefits for 6G   70
Blockchains and Robots   71
Blockchain-Enabled Trust Game   72
Open Research Challenges   72
Experimenter Smart Contract   75

Blockchain Mechanism Deposit 76
Experimental Setup 77
Results 77
On-Chaining Oracle for Networked *N*-Player Trust Game 79
Architecture of Oracle 79
On-Chaining of Voting-Based Decisions 81
Results 81
Robonomics: Playing The *N*-Player Trust Game with
Persuasive Robots 83
Robonomics: Key Principles 83
Persuasive Robotics Strategies 84
Experimental Setup 86
Results 88
Conclusions 89
Notes 89
References 90

5 **From Superorganism to Stigmergic Society &
Collective Intelligence in the 6G Era** **92**
Introduction 92
Society 5.0: From Robonomics to Tokenomics 96
The Path (DAO) to a Human-Centered Society 98
Purpose-Driven Tokens and Token Engineering 98
Token Engineering DAO Framework for Society 5.0 99
The Human Use of Human Beings: Cybernetics
and Society 101
From Superorganism to Stigmergic Society and Collective
Intelligence In The 6G Era 102
Implementation and Experimental Results 104
Conclusions 107
Notes 108
References 108

Conclusions **110**
Summary 110
Notes 113

Index 114

Acknowledgment

The completion of this book would have never been possible without the support and collaboration of a number of amazing people. I would like to thank my former advisor Prof. Martin Maier of the Institut National de la Recherche Scientifique (INRS), Montréal, Canada for outstanding support and guidance in my initial academic and scientific steps. Furthermore, I would like to thank Dr. Amin Ebrahimzadeh and Dr. Sajjad Rostami for their fruitful collaboration to the experimental results reported in Chapters 3, 4, and 5 of this book. At CRC Press, I would like to thank Daina Habdankaite and Laura Piedrahita for their guidance throughout the whole process of preparing the book. I would like to acknowledge the Natural Sciences and Engineering Research Council of Canada (NSERC) for funding our research. Finally, and most importantly, I would like to take this opportunity to express my great depth of gratitude to my parents and friends for their endless support, love, and encouragement.

List of Acronyms

1G	First Generation
2G	Second Generation
3G	Third Generation
4G	Fourth Generation
5G	Fifth Generation
6G	Sixth Generation
6Genesis	6G Enabled Smart Society and Ecosystem
6GFP	6Genesis Flagship Program
ABI	Application Binary Interface
ACC	Access Control Contract
ACK	Acknowledgment
AGI	Artificial General Intelligence
AI	Artificial Intelligence
AMM	Automated Market Making
ANN	Artificial Neural Network
API	Application Programming Interface
APT	Advanced Persistent Threat
AR	Augmented Reality
AWS	Amazon Web Services
B5G	Beyond 5G
BIoT	Blockchain-based IoT
BS	Base Station
CCSC	Crypto Currency Smart Card (CCSC)
CI	Collective Intelligence
CoC	Computation Oriented Communication
CoMP	Coordinated MultiPoint
CoZ	Crowd-of-Oz
CPS	Cyber-Physical Systems
CPSS	Cyber-Physical-Social Systems
CPU	Central Processing Unit
CTS	Clear To Send
CV	Computer Vision
DApps	Decentralized Applications
DAO	Decentralized Autonomous Organization

DCF	Distributed Coordination Function
DEX	Decentralized Exchanges
DIFS	DCF Interframe Space
DLT	Distributed Ledger Technology
DNS	Domain Name System
DSOC	Decentralized Self-Organizing Cooperative
DVB	Digital Video Broadcasting
ECDSA	Elliptic Curve Digital Signature Algorithm
e-Deliveries	Registered Electronic Delivery Services
eMBB	enhanced Mobile Broadband
EOA	Externally Owned Account
EPON	Ethernet Passive Optical Network
ERC	Ethereum Request for Comments
ESF	Edge Sample Forecast
ESPN	ExtraSensory Perception Network
ETSI	European Telecommunications Standards Institute
EVM	Ethereum Virtual Machine
FiWi	Fiber-Wireless
GSM	Global System for Mobile Communications
GWAP	Games With A Purpose
H2H	Human-to-Human
H2M	Human-to-Machine
H2R	Human-to-Robot
HABA/MABA	Humans-Are-Better-At/Machines-Are-Better-At
HART	Human-Agent-Robot Teamwork
HCI	Human-Computer Interfaces
HetNets	Heterogenous Networks
HIT	Human Intelligence Task
HITL	Human-In-The-Loop
HO	Human Operator
HRI	Human-Robot Interaction
HSI	Human System Interface
HTML	HyperText Markup Language
IA	Intelligence Amplification
ICO	Initial Coin Offering
ICT	Information and Communications Technology
IFrame	Inline Frame
IoE	Internet of Everything
IoT	Internet of Things
IP	Internet Protocol
IPFS	Inter-Planetary File System
ITU	International Telecommunication Union

JC	Judge Contract
KPI	Key Performance Indicators
LED	Light-Emitting Diode
LLL	Lisp Like Language
LoRa	Long Range
LPWA	Low-Power Wide-Area
LTE-A	LTE-Advanced
M2M	Machine-to-Machine
MAP	Mesh Access Point
MEC	Multi-access Edge Computing
MIMO	Multiple-Input Multiple-Output
mMTC	massive Machine Type Communications
mmWave	millimeter-Wave
MP	Mesh Point
MPP	Mesh Portal Point
MR	Mobile Robot
MTurk	Amazon Mechanical Turk
MU	Mobile User
NAT	Network Address Translation
NFT	Non-Fungible Token
NOMA	Non-Orthogonal Multiple Access
OFDM	Orthogonal Frequency Division Multiplexing
OLT	Optical Line Terminal
ONU	Optical Network Unit
P2P	Peer-to-Peer
PHY	Physical Layer
PON	Passive Optical Networks
PoS	Proof-of-State
PoW	Proof-of-Work
QR	Quick Response
RACS	Remote APDU Call Secure
RAN	Radio Access Network
RF	Radio Frequency
RFID	Radio Frequency Identification
RPC	Remote Procedure Call
RSS	Really Simple Syndication
RTS	Request To Send
SHA	Secure Hash Algorithm
sHRI	social Human-Robot Interaction
SIFS	Short Interframe Space
SLA	Service Level Agreement
SMS	Short Message Service

SSI	Self-Sovereign Identity
TDM	Time Division Multiplexing
TLD	Top-Level Domain
TOR	Teleoperator Robot
URL	Uniform Resource Locator
URLLC	Ultra-Reliable Low-Latency Communications
VPN	Virtual Private Network
WDM	Wavelength Division Multiplexing
WLAN	Wireless Local Area Network
WOBANs	Wireless-Optical Broadband Access Networks
WOR	WiFi Offloading Ratio
WoZ	Wizard-of-Oz
XR	Extended Reality

6G-Blockchain Vision and Research Directions

1

BACKGROUND AND MOTIVATION

Evolution of Mobile Networks and Internet

The general evolution of global mobile network standards was first to maximize coverage in the first and second generations and then to maximize capacity in the third and fourth generations. In addition to higher capacity, research on fifth generation (5G) mobile networks has focused on lower end-to-end latency, higher spectral efficiency and energy efficiency, and more connection nodes [1]. More specifically, the first generation (1G) mobile network was designed for voice services with a data rate of up to 2.4 kbit/s. It used analog signals to transmit information, and there was no universal wireless standard. Conversely, second generation (2G) was based on digital modulation technologies and offered data rates of up to 384 kbit/s, supporting not only voice services but also data services such as short message service (SMS). The dominant 2G standard was the global system for mobile (GSM) communication. The third generation (3G) mobile network provided a data rate of at least 2 Mbit/s and enabled advanced services, including web browsing, TV streaming, and video services. For achieving global roaming, 3GPP was established to define technical specifications and mobile standards. Fourth generation (4G) mobile networks were introduced in the late 2000s. 4G is an all-Internet Protocol (IP) based network, which is capable of providing high-speed data rates of up to 1 Gbit/s in the downlink and 500 Mbit/s in the uplink in support of advanced applications like digital video broadcasting (DVB), high-definition TV content, and video chat. LTE-Advanced (LTE-A) has been the dominant 4G standard, which integrates techniques such as

DOI: 10.1201/9781003427322-1

coordinated multipoint (CoMP) transmission and reception, multiple-input multiple-output (MIMO), and orthogonal frequency division multiplexing (OFDM) [2]. The main goal of 5G has been to use not only the microwave band but also the millimeter-wave (mm-wave) band for the first time in order to significantly increase data rates up to 10 Gbit/s [3]. Another feature of 5G is a more efficient use of the spectrum, as measured by increasing the number of bits per Hertz [4]. ITU's International Mobile Telecommunications 2020 (IMT 2020) standard proposed the following three major 5G usage scenarios:

1. Enhanced mobile broadband (Embb)
2. Ultra-reliable and low latency communications (URLLC)
3. Massive machine-type communications (mMTC) [5]

One of the most interesting 5G low-latency applications is the emerging Tactile Internet that envisages realizing *haptic communications* and thereby enabling users to not only see and hear but also touch and manipulate remote physical and/or virtual objects through the Internet [6, 7]. The Tactile Internet, which is driven by recent advancements in computerization, automation, and robotization, is expected to significantly augment human-machine interaction, thereby converting today's content delivery networks into skillset/labor delivery networks [8–10]. The Tactile Internet holds promise to create new entrepreneurial opportunities and jobs, which are expected to have a profound socioeconomic impact on almost every segment of our everyday life with use cases ranging from augmented/virtual reality (AR/VR) and autonomous driving to healthcare and smart grid. Many of these industry verticals (e.g., AR/VR, telediagnosis, telesurgery, and telepresence) require very low latency and ultra-high reliability for realizing ultra-responsive interactive applications such as bilateral teleoperation/telepresence. Note, however, that some use cases which do not necessarily require mobility all the time can be realized over fixed broadband networks. This suggests that future cellular networks need to be fully converged networks, allowing for a flexible selection of different fixed and mobile access technologies while sharing core network functionalities [11].

Interactive systems, including in particular AR/VR and teleoperation, demand an ultra-low round-trip latency of 1–10 ms together with high reliability. The high availability and security, ultra-fast and highly reliable response times and carrier-grade reliability of the Tactile Internet will add a new dimension to the interaction of humans with machines/robots. To gain a more profound understanding of the Tactile Internet, it may be helpful to compare it to the emerging Internet of Things (IoT) and 5G mobile networks. While the concept of IoT is far from novel and goes back to 1995, it is only recently that we are experiencing a rapidly increasing growth of interest in IoT from

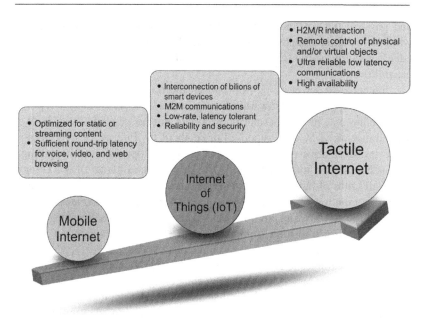

FIGURE 1.1 Revolutionary leap of the Tactile Internet in compliance with ITU-T Technology Watch Report.

both industry and academia. Figure 1.1 depicts the revolutionary leap of the Tactile Internet in compliance with the ITU-T[1] Technology Watch Report on the Tactile Internet [12]. While the ultra-fast response time and carrier-grade reliability of the Tactile Internet will add a new dimension to human-machine interaction, emerging 5G networks have to handle an unprecedented growth of mobile data traffic as well as an enormous volume of data from smart sensors and actuators, the empowering elements of the IoT.

The difference between the Tactile Internet and IoT may be best expressed in terms of underlying communications paradigms and enabling end devices. The Tactile Internet involves the inherent human-in-the-loop (HITL) nature of human-to-machine interaction, whereas the IoT is centered around autonomous machine-to-machine (M2M) communications without any interaction with humans. The Tactile Internet relies on human-to-machine/robot (H2M/R) interaction and thus allows for a human-centric design approach towards creating novel immersive experiences, expanding humans' capabilities through the Internet. Furthermore, the Tactile Internet may be viewed as an extension of immersive VR from a virtual to a physical environment. It allows for the tactile steering and control of not only virtual but also real objects, e.g., teleoperated robots. The boundary between virtual (i.e., online) and physical (i.e., offline) worlds is to become increasingly imperceptible, while both digital and physical capabilities of humans are to be extended via edge computing variants, ideally with embedded artificial intelligence (AI) capabilities.

Recently, Maier et al. [13] introduced the *Internet of No Things* as an important stepping stone toward ushering in the sixth generation (6G) post-smartphone era, in which smartphones may not be needed anymore. We argued that while 5G was supposed to be about the Internet of Everything, to be transformative 6G might be just about the opposite of Everything, that is, Nothing or, more technically, No Things. The Internet of No Things offers all kinds of human-intended services without owning or carrying any type of computing or storage devices. It envisions Internet services appearing from the surrounding environment when needed and disappearing when not needed. The transition from the current gadgets-based Internet to the Internet of No Things is divided into three phases: (*i*) bearables (e.g., smartphone), (*ii*) wearables (e.g., Google and Levi's smart jacket), and then finally *(iii)* nearables. Nearables denote nearby computing/storage technologies and service provisioning mechanisms that are intelligent enough to learn and react according to user context and history in order to provide user-intended services.

Joseph A. Paradiso [14] outlined his pioneering work on extrasensory perception (ESP) in an IoT context at MIT Media Lab. The authors showed that in a sensor-driven world, network-connected sensors embedded in anything function as extensions of the human nervous system and enable us to enter the long-predicted era of ubiquitous computing as envisioned by Mark Weiser more than a quarter of a century ago. In "The Computer for the 21st Century," Mark Weiser argued that the most profound technologies are those that disappear. They weave themselves into the fabric of everyday life until they are indistinguishable from it [15]. This is now widely referred to as ubiquitous computing, though Mark Weiser called it *embodied virtuality* originally.

Figure 1.2 depicts the architecture of our proposed extrasensory perception network (ESPN), which integrates the following three evolutionary stages of mobile computing: (*i*) ubiquitous, (*ii*) pervasive, and (*iii*) persuasive computing. Ubiquitous computing is embedded in the things surrounding us (i.e., nearables), while pervasive computing involves our bearables and wearables. Persuasive computing aims at changing the behavior of users through social influence. An interesting phenomenon for changing behavior in an online virtual environment is known as the "Proteus effect," were the behavior of individuals is shaped by the characteristics and traits of their virtual avatars, especially through interaction during inter-avatar events. The underlying physical network infrastructure, which is illustrated in Fig. 1.2, consists

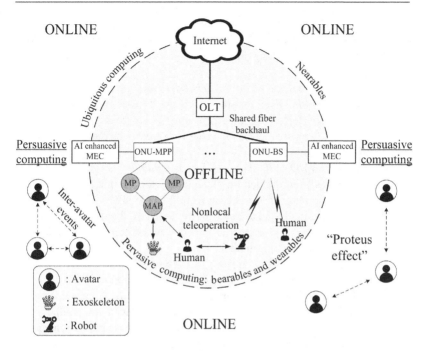

FIGURE 1.2 Extrasensory perception network (ESPN) architecture integrating the three evolutionary stages of mobile computing: (*i*) ubiquitous, (*ii*) pervasive, and (*iii*) persuasive computing.

of a fiber backhaul shared by WLAN mesh portal points (MPPs) and cellular base stations (BSs) that are collocated with optical network units (ONUs), which in turn are connected to the central optical line terminal (OLT) of the fiber backhaul. Based on real-world haptic traces, we studied the use case of nonlocal teleoperation between a human operator (HO) and teleoperator robot (TOR), which are both physical (i.e., offline) entities (Fig. 1.2). Further, Maier and Ebrahimzadeh [16] showed that AI-enhanced MEC helps decouple haptic feedback from the impact of extensive propagation delays by forecasting delayed or lost haptic feedback samples. This enables humans to perceive remote task environments in real-time at a 1 ms granularity.

6G Vision

As 5G is entering the commercial deployment phase, research has started to focus on 6G mobile networks, which are anticipated to be deployed by 2030 [17–19]. Typically, next-generation systems do not emerge from the vacuum, but follow the industrial and technological trends from previous generations. Potential research directions of 6G consistent with these trends were provided in [20], including among others:

- *6G will continue to move to higher frequencies with wider system bandwidth*: Given that the spectrum at lower frequencies has almost been depleted, the current trend is to obtain wider bandwidth at higher frequencies in order to increase the data rate more than 10 times.

- *Massive MIMO will remain a key technology for 6G*: Massive MIMO has been the defining technology for 5G that has enabled the antenna number to increase from 2 to 64. Given that the performance gains have saturated in the areas of channel coder and modulator, the hope of increasing spectral efficiency for 6G will remain in the multiple antenna area.

- *6G will take the cloud service to the next level*: With the ever-higher data rates, short delays, and low transmission costs, many of the computational and storage functions have been moved from the smartphone to the cloud. As a result, most of the computational power of the smartphone can focus on presentation rendering, making VR, AR, or extended reality (XR) more impressive and affordable. Many AI services that are intrinsically cloud-based may prevail more easily and broadly. In addition to smartphones, less expensive functional terminals may once again flourish, providing growth opportunities in more application areas.

- *Grant-free transmissions could be more prominent in 6G*: In past cellular network generations, transmissions were primarily based on a grant-oriented design with strong centralized system control. More advanced grant-free protocols and approaches will be needed for 6G. It is possible that the non-orthogonal multiple access (NOMA) technology may have another opportunity to prevail due to its short delay performance even though it failed to take off during the 5G time period.

- *mMTC is more likely to take shape in the older generation before it can succeed in the next generation*: mMTC has been one of the major directions for the next-generation system design since the market growth of communications between people has saturated. High expectations have been put on 5G mMTC to deliver significant growth for the cellular industry. Until now, however, this expectation has been mismatched with the reality on the ground. Therefore, the current trend appears to indicate that mMTC would be more likely to prevail by utilizing older technology that operates in a lower band.

• *6G will transform a transmission network into a computing network*: One of the possible trademarks of 6G could be the harmonious operations of transmission, computing, AI, machine learning, and big data analytics such that 6G is expected to detect the users' transmission intent autonomously and automatically provide personalized services based on a user's intent and desire.

In September 2019, the world's first 6G white paper was published as an outcome of the first 6G wireless summit, which was held in Levi, Finland, earlier in March 2019 with almost 300 participants from 29 countries, including major infrastructure manufacturers, operators, regulators as well as academia [21]. Each year, the white paper will be updated following the annual 6G wireless summit. While 5G was primarily developed to address the anticipated capacity growth demand from consumers and to enable the increasing importance of the IoT, 6G will require a substantially more holistic approach, embracing a much wider community. Further, 6G will become more human-centered than 5G, which primarily focused on industry verticals. Putting people at the center of a future super-smart society lies also at the heart of the recently emerging concept of Society 5.0 [22].

Many of the key performance indicators (KPIs) used for 5G are valid also for 6G. However, beyond 5G (B5G) and 6G, KPIs in most of the technology domains once again point to an increase by a factor of 10–100, though a 1000 times price reduction from the customer's viewpoint may be also key to the success of 6G [23]. Note that cost reduction is particularly important for providing connectivity to rural and underprivileged areas, where the cost of backhaul deployment is the major limitation. According to Yaacoub and Alouini [24], providing rural connectivity represents a key 6G challenge and opportunity given that around half of the world's population lives in rural or underprivileged areas. Among other important KPIs, 6G is expected to be the first wireless standard to exceed a peak throughput of 1 Tbit/s per user.

Arguably more interestingly, 6G envisions that totally new services such as telepresence, as a surrogate for actual travel, will be made possible by combinations of graphical representations (e.g., avatars), wearable displays, mobile robots and drones, specialized processors, and next-generation wireless networks. Similarly, smartphones are likely to be replaced by pervasive XR experiences through lightweight glasses, whereby feedback will be provided to other senses via earphones and haptic interfaces. Furthermore, 6G needs a network with embedded trust given that the digital and physical worlds will be deeply entangled by 2030. Toward this end, blockchain also known as distributed ledger technology (DLT) may play a major role in 6G networks due to its capability to establish and maintain trust in a distributed fashion without requiring any central authority.

Blockchain and Distributed Ledger Technologies

The radical potential of blockchain technology has long spread outside the world of crypto into the hand of the general public. We've all heard through one way or another that it is most likely the most revolutionary technology that is presently available in any known market and that includes the real world as well as the digital space. Blockchain technology is principally behind the emergence of Bitcoin [25] and many other cryptocurrencies that are too numerous to mention [26]. A blockchain is essentially a distributed database of records (or public ledger) of all transactions or digital events that have been executed and shared among participating parties [27]. Each transaction in the public ledger is verified by consensus between the majority of the participants in the system. Once entered, information can never be erased. The blockchain contains a certain and verifiable record of every single transaction ever made. At the point when the block reaches a certain size, it is timestamped and linked to the previous block through a cryptographic hash, thereby forming a chain of timestamped blocks (hence the name blockchain), as depicted in Fig. 1.3.

Blockchain technology is being successfully applied in both financial and non-financial applications. It has the potential to reduce the role of one of the most important economic and regulatory actors in our society, the middleman [28, 29]. Blockchain technology was initially linked to the decentralized cryptocurrency Bitcoin, as it is the main and first application of the network (known as Blockchain 1.0 [30]). However, there exist many other use cases and several hundred different applications besides Bitcoin that use blockchain technology as a platform such as Ethereum.

Ethereum is a type of open software platform that runs on blockchain technology. At its heart lies the so-called Ethereum Virtual Machine (EVM), which is capable of executing code of arbitrary algorithmic complexity [31]. The Ethereum platform can be used not only as a cryptocurrency but also to allow developers to write smart contracts, and program codes stored on a blockchain that are executed when predetermined conditions are met. Ethereum smart contracts allow end-users to interact with next-generation decentralized applications (DApps). As opposed to traditional centralized applications, where the backend code is running on

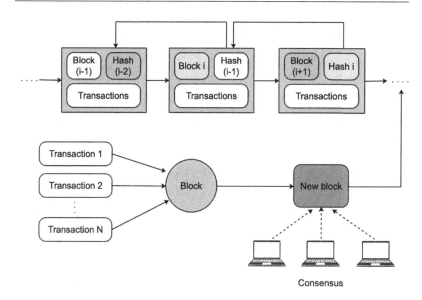

FIGURE 1.3 A graphical representation of blockchain transaction workflow.

centralized servers, DApps are apps whose server-client models are decentralized. DApps run on blockchain networks without a central authority and use decentralized storage protocols. DApps may be used in many other fields by making the process of creating applications much easier and more efficient. For instance, they can be used for realizing non-financial blockchain DApps (e.g., IoT device registration DApp, blockchain-based digital identity application). The rise of Ethereum and smart contracts heralded Blockchain 2.0 [30].

As the hype of blockchain technology advanced, Blockchain 3.0 aims to popularize blockchain-based solutions expanding the traditional sectors (finance, goods transactions, and so on) to government, IoT, decentralized AI, supply chain management, smart energy, health, data management, and education [32, 33]. Therefore, the applications of blockchain have evolved to much wider scopes. However, these new applications introduce new features to the next-generation platforms including key aspects such as platforms interconnection or more advanced smart contracts that provide higher levels of transparency while reducing bureaucracy with self-enforcing code. These new technologies, therefore, promise more decentralized and spontaneous coordination over the Internet between users who do not know or trust each other, often referred to as decentralized autonomous organizations (DAO). DAO exists as open-source, distributed software for executing smart contracts

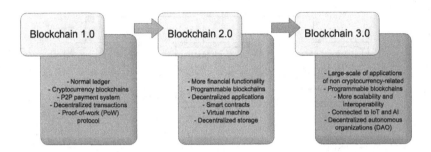

FIGURE 1.4   Evolution of blockchain technology.

built within the Ethereum project. DAO is like a decentralized organization, except that autonomous software agents (i.e., smart contracts) make the decisions, not humans. In a more decentralized setup, the governance rules automatically steer behavior with tokenized incentives and disincentives [34]. In such cases, programmable assets called tokens managed by a special smart contract act as governance rules to incentivize and steer a network of actors without centralized intermediaries [34]. Further, the tokens issued by the DAO enable their respective holders to vote on matters about the development of the organization and make decisions. As a result, the decision-taking process is automated and a consensus is reached among the participants. For illustration, Fig. 1.4 depicts the evolution of blockchain technology from Blockchain 1.0 to 3.0.

The introduction of smart contracts to the blockchain has added programmability to this disruptive technology and has changed the software ecosystem by removing third parties for the administration of (non) business purposes. Although promising, smart contracts and blockchain do not have access to the information outside of their networks (i.e., off-chain data). The blockchain in fact is an enclosed system where interactions are limited to the data available on it. Hence, it is still an open practical problem referred to as the "oracle problem" that is defined as how real-world data can be transferred into/from the blockchain [35]. Toward this end, oracles (also known as data feeds) act as trusted third-party services that send and verify external information and submit it to smart contracts to trigger state changes in the blockchain [36]. Oracles may not only relay information to the smart contracts but also send it to external resources. They are simply contracts on the blockchain for serving data requests by other contracts. Without oracles, smart contracts would have limited connectivity; hence, they are vital for the blockchain ecosystem due to broadening the scope of smart contracts operation.

ADVANCED BLOCKCHAIN TECHNOLOGIES: PRIOR ART AND RECENT PROGRESS

In this section, we review prior research work related to advanced blockchain technologies and, after classifying them into three separate yet interdependent categories, we discuss each one in greater detail. The main branches of our classification are DAO, blockchain oracles, and token engineering.

DAO

The last few years have seen the emergence of DAO in the field of blockchain as a new form for running organizations on the Internet. DAO is novel socio-technical systems that enable a new way of online coordination and decision-making. DAO as a new form of online governance are collections of smart contracts deployed on a blockchain platform that intercede groups of members (humans or machines). In short, DAO may be defined as a group of members with common goals that join under a blockchain infrastructure that enforces a set of shared rules. Typically, the members of a DAO are registered, each with a unique address. They also have a number of governance tokens linked to that address, which are usually required for participation and may play a role in the DAO decision-making process. It is also common that DAO manage resources, e.g., cryptocurrencies, whereby DAO members may decide how to allocate them through a decision system.

The first remarkable DAO was *The DAO*, launched in April 2016 by a group of programmers. The DAO was a sort of hedge fund, in which contributors could directly vote for proposed projects. Investors would exchange Ether for tokens during an Initial Coin Offering (ICO). Then investors would vote for new projects with their votes or tokens. In June 2016, due to an error in The DAO code, an attacker robbed a large part of its funds [37]. Another example of DAO on decentralized finance (DeFi) is MakerDAO², which began in 2015. MakerDAO aims to bring financial stability and transparency to the world economy. This community governs the Maker Protocol, which defines the use of the Dai token, a stable cryptocurrency that avoids financial risk when Ethereum's cryptocurrency value fluctuates. A variety of DAO platforms have recently emerged to facilitate the deployment of DAO in the blockchain by significantly reducing the technological knowledge required and providing DAO software as a service. These DAO platforms enable users with sufficient knowledge on how blockchains work and how to create a DAO using a template that typically can be customized.

The main platforms are Aragon[3], DAOstack[4], and Colony[5], as explained in more detail in the following:

- *Aragon:* Aragon is by far the largest DAO platform. Aragon provides a static template to make one's own DAO, but it also allows one to create a customized one. The template sets a special token, which is used by a small group of members to take decisions, like accepting new members. The other key feature that Aragon introduces are permissions, which serve as an access control system intended to safely connect apps and entities (users or other apps) together. Initially, the DAO creator has the permissions to manage it, but usually, the creator transfers those permissions to the voting app such that the DAO is managed through voting. This enables more democratic decentralized governance models.

- *DAOstack:* Unlike Aragon, the DAOstack platform does not offer many customizations. Among others, they currently provide a single decision-making system for all their DAOs. This voting system, called *holographic consensus* [38], aims to solve the problems of scaling a DAO. In holographic consensus, the quorum required to approve a proposal can be reduced from absolute majority to relative majority if some conditions are met. The most significant condition concerns the predictors or stakers, who are not necessarily members of any DAO. Those predictors can stake a special token called *GEN* to predict the result of a proposal. If stakers are right, they are rewarded, whereas if they fail, they lose their stake. Regarding the proposal, if the staked amount reaches a specific limit, then the quorum of that proposal will be reduced to a relative majority. As a result, stakers help DAO to highlight meaningful proposals and make a profit if their services are useful. In practice, this behavior mimics a prediction market [39].

- *Colony:* Colony has been the latest and recently released DAO platform that enables the creation of DAO, or "colonies," as they named them. Colony's DAO are shared by people with common goals and resources to accomplish them, though these DAOs can be split into domains or even sub-domains with more specific purposes[6]. Those purposes are translated into tasks that DAO members may accomplish to gain more influence. On the other hand, DAO members may have a reputation token and the only way to obtain more is by performing tasks, which can also be exchanged by non-reputational tokens like Ethereum's native cryptocurrency Ether. Unlike Aragon or DAOstack, which are vote-driven and use voting systems to allocate resources, Colony has a meritocratic system because the only way to increase the members' influence is to work for the organization [40]. By avoiding to vote, all decisions are approved by default unless someone has an objection, in which case it is discussed and resolved via voting.

Blockchain Oracles

Blockchain oracles can be classified depending on a number of different qualities: (*i*) *source,* i.e., the origin of data, (*ii*) *direction of information,* i.e., inbound or outbound from the viewpoint of the blockchain, (*iii*) *the initiator of the data flow,* whether it is push- or pull-based communication, (iv) trust, i.e., centralized or decentralized, and (v) design pattern.

Oracle data sources can range from (*i*) *software oracles,* where data comes from online sources (e.g., online web servers or database), (*ii*) *hardware oracles,* where data comes from the physical world (e.g., IoT devices, robots), and (*iii*) *human oracles,* in which an individual with specialized knowledge/skills in a particular field can play the role of the oracle. They can research and verify the authenticity of information from various sources and translate that information into smart contracts. Since human oracles can verify their identity using cryptography, the possibility of a fraudster faking their identity and providing corrupted data is relatively very low.

Direction of information means the way information flows, i.e., from or to external resources with respect to the initiator of the data flow. Toward this end, there are four combinations of these options: (*i*) *pull-based inbound oracle,* when the on-chain component requests the off-chain state from an off-chain component, (*ii*) *pull-based outbound oracle,* when the off-chain component retrieves the on-chain state from an on-chain component, (*iii*) *push-based inbound oracle,* when the off-chain component sends the off-chain state to the on-chain component, (*iv*) *push-based outbound oracle,* when the on-chain component sends the off-chain state to an off-chain component.

Further, there is the concept of trust that can be centralized or decentralized. *Centralized oracles* are efficient but they can be risky because a single entity provides information, controls the oracles, and a failure makes the contracts less resilient to vulnerabilities and attacks. In contrast, *decentralized oracles* (i.e., consensus-based oracles) increase the reliability of the information provided to smart contracts by querying multiple resources. It should be noted that an oracle is considered decentralized if it is permissionless such that users can join or leave, and every user has equal rights [41]. Finally, oracles design patterns are defined as (*i*) *request-response,* when the data space is huge and can be implemented as on-chain smart contracts and initiated on-chain or off-chain oracles for monitoring, retrieving, and returning data, (*ii*) *publish-subscribe,* when the data is expected to change, e.g., really simple syndication (RSS) feeds, and (*iii*) *immediate read,* when the data is required for an immediate decision.

There exist many commercial and open-source tools that implement inbound oracles. *Orisi*[7] is a solution for a distributed set of inbound oracles for Bitcoin, which are executed by independent and trustworthy third parties. The majority of all oracles have to agree on the outcome from external data. To fulfill this purpose, money from senders and receivers is parked at a multiple-signature address, including all signatures as well as the signature address. Orisi is categorized as a pull-based inbound oracle. Oraclize, recently rebranded as *Provable Things*[8] is a popular service for inbound oracles that works with multiple smart contracts enabled blockchain platforms. The service acts like a trusted intermediary between blockchains and a variety of independent data sources. Its Provable Engine executes a set of instructions to react as certain conditions are met, thus making it classifiable both as a push-based and a pull-based inbound oracle.

Reality Keys provides a combination of both automated and human-driven pull-based inbound oracles [42]. *Chainlink*[9] offers a general-purpose framework for building decentralized inbound oracles, providing decentralization on both oracle and data-source levels. A Chainlink node can have multiple external adapters for different data sources. *Witnet* provides a decentralized oracle network protocol based on Ethereum [43]. It also enables miners to earn tokens. An Ethereum bridge is implemented, providing Witnet nodes to run Ethereum nodes with the option to operate with Ether and make contract calls.

Blockchain inbound oracles have also been considered in a number of research works. Xu et al. introduce the concept of *validation oracles*, namely trusted third-party operators (either automatic or human) that act as inbound oracles [44]. The authors distinguish between internal ones, periodically transmitting externally verified data to the blockchain, and external ones, operating as trusted external validators of transactions based on information that is external to the blockchain. According to our scheme, we see that the former is push-based and the latter is pull-based. Among the pioneering research works in the field of oracles is ASTRAEA introduced by Adler et al. as a decentralized pull-based inbound oracle service [45]. The implementation provides a voting game, which decides the truth or inaccuracy of propositions. Players can be voters or certifiers. While certifiers play a role in cases with the requirement for high accuracy, voters are utilized for low-risk/low-reward roles. Zhang et al. present *Town Crier*, a push-based inbound oracle that acts like a data-feed system connecting a blockchain with a back-end that scrapes secure websites [46].

More interestingly, Heiss et al. provide a set of key requirements for trustworthy data on-chaining, explaining the challenges and the solutions for them [47]. They argue that in addition to safety and liveness as the characteristics of distributed systems, truthfulness is necessary as it prevents the execution of blockchain state transition from untruthful data provisioning. Based on these properties. Challenges are defined for each of them as availability, correctness, and incentive compatibility. Incentive compatibility consists of two key characteristics: (i) attributability referred to as mapping data to the source provider, and with respect to the behavior, the data source can be rewarded or penalized, and (ii) accountability defined as depositing stake before providing data, and upon the truthful data provisioning, it is paid back. Correctness consists of authenticity and integrity such that the former deals with approving the data source and the latter shows the data should become untampered during the transition, respectively. Finally, liveness refers to availability and accessibility such that the former implies that the availability of the system should be as good as of its least available component i.e., the outage should be kept minimum. The latter means that data must be accessible at any time.

Token Engineering

Tokens have emerged with the introduction of *Web3* [34]. While Web1 allowed everyone to share ideas and Web2 allowed communities to form and discuss those ideas, Web3 enables those communities to leverage financial capital and go from discussions to tangible action. At their core, tokens are entries in distributed ledgers that are assigned to blockchain accounts and for which transactions require authorization, thereby authenticity and preventing modification and tampering without consent. Tokens are designed in a customized way by using a token template that can be extended or instantiated. Tokens can be understood as an asset that resides on the blockchain, which can be stored or managed using Ethereum addresses and special smart contracts. There are various types of tokens that can be built on Ethereum, usually used in DApps and followed an existing standard. The most popular tokens standards are described below:

- *ERC-20 Standard[10]:* ERC-20 tokens can be defined as a group of identical tokens (i.e., fungible tokens), all with the same properties. They follow the ERC-20 standard which includes a common set of rules for creating and managing fungible tokens. The use of

ERC-20 tokens enables the creation of small economies that have liquid markets for different use cases. ERC-20 tokens can be traded on multiple types of platforms such as regular exchanges, decentralized exchanges (DEX), which is a peer-to-peer (P2P) marketplace that connects cryptocurrency buyers and sellers, or with an automated liquidity pool that enables seamless token swaps using an automated market making (AMM) algorithms to determine the price of ERC-20 tokens.

- *ERC-721 Standard[11]:* ERC-721 tokens are non-fungible tokens (NFT). This implies that each token has a unique set of properties and values associated with it. The ERC-721 standard is an interface that each smart contract that creates ERC-721 tokens has to implement. There are multiple functions that enable interactions with NFTs such as finding the owner address of an ERC-721 token or approving the transfer of an ERC-721 token. ERC-721 tokens have found applicability in many domains of the Ethereum space, the most relevant being gaming, arts, collectibles items, utilities, and VR real estate[12]. ERC-721 tokens can also change ownership and be traded for other tokens or Ether. However, the way this is done is different. Since all ERC-721 tokens have unique properties, AMM algorithms are not feasible to be implemented.

- *ERC-1155 Standard[13]:* ERC-1155 is a new token proposal standard aimed at creating both fungible and non-fungible tokens in the same contract. This could be particularly useful for games that want to create more complex in-game economies.

FROM INDUSTRY 4.0 TOWARD SOCIETY 5.0

Cyber-Physical-Social Systems (CPSS)

Smart factories under Industry 4.0 have several benefits such as optimal resource handling, but also imply minimum human intervention in manufacturing. When human beings are functionally integrated into a cyber-physical-social (CPS) at the social, cognitive, and physical levels, it becomes a so-called cyber-physical-social systems (CPSS), whose members may engage in CPS behaviors that eventually enable metahuman beings with diverse types of superhuman capabilities. CPSS belongs to the family of future techno-social systems that by design still require heavy involvement from humans at the network edge instead of automating them away. For a comprehensive survey of the state of the art of CPSS, we refer the interested reader to [49].

Industry 5.0

Recently, in January 2021, the European Commission released the first edition of their policy brief on Industry 5.0 [48]. Industry 5.0 will be defined by a re-found and widened purposefulness, going beyond producing goods and services for profit. A purely profit-driven approach has become increasingly untenable. In a globalized world, a narrow focus on profit fails to account correctly for environmental and societal costs and benefits. Further, crises such as the Covid-19 pandemic highlighted the fragility of our current approach to globalized production, especially where value chains serve basic human needs, e.g., healthcare. This wider purpose constitutes three core elements: (i) human-centricity, (ii) sustainability, and (iii) resilience.

One of the most important paradigmatic transitions characterizing Industry 5.0 is the shift of focus from technology-driven progress to a thoroughly human-centric approach. An important prerequisite for Industry 5.0 is that technology serves people, rather than the other way around, by expanding the capabilities of workers (up-skilling and re-skilling) with innovative technological means such as VR/AR tools, mobile robots, and exoskeletons.

Currently, two visions emerge for Industry 5.0. The first one is human–robot co-working, where humans will focus on tasks requiring creativity, and robots will do the rest. The second vision for Industry 5.0 is bioeconomy, i.e., a holistic approach toward the smart use of biological resources for industrial processes [50]. The bioeconomy has established itself worldwide as a mainstay for achieving a sustainable economy. Its success is based on our understanding of biological processes and principles that help revolutionize our economy dominated by fossil resources and create a suitable framework so that the economy, ecology, and society are perceived as necessary single entities and not as rivals. More specifically, biologization will be the guiding principle of the bioeconomy. Biologization takes advantage of nature's efficiency for economic purposes—whether they be plants, animals, residues, or natural organisms. Almost every discipline shares promising interfaces with biology. In the long term, biologization will be just as significant as a cross-cutting approach as digitalization already is today. Biologization will pave the way for Industry 5.0 in the same way as digitalization triggered Industry 4.0. It is also obvious that the two trends—biologization and digitalization—will be mutually beneficial [51].

It is interesting to note that in [48], the authors also elaborate on the relation between the concepts of Industry 5.0 and Society 5.0. While both concepts are related in the sense that they refer to a fundamental shift of our society and economy towards a new paradigm, Society 5.0 is not restricted to the manufacturing sector but addresses larger social challenges based on the integration of physical and virtual spaces. In the subsequent sections, we further elaborate on the Society 5.0 vision and present an illustrative use case of biologization.

Society 5.0

The Industrial Revolution reduced the agricultural population from more than 90 percent to less than 5 percent. Similarly, the IT revolution reduced the manufacturing population from more than 70 percent to approximately 15 percent. The Intelligence Revolution of the 6G era will reduce the entire service population to less than 10 percent. Upon the question of where will people go and what will they do then, the author of [52] gives the following answer: Gaming! Not leisure, but scientific gaming in cyberspace. Artificial societies, computational experiments, and parallel execution—the so-called ACP approach—may form the scientific foundation, while CPSS platforms may be the enabling infrastructure for the emergence of intelligent industries. In the ACP approach, intelligent industries will build all kinds of artificial societies, organizations, and systems in order to perform different types of computational experiments and conduct numerous scientific games for analyzing, evaluating, and optimizing decision-making processes, as well as mastering skills and resources required for the completion of tasks in the shortest time with the least energy and cost through the parallel execution of and interaction between real and artificial dual entities, who we can play, work, and live with. Everything will have its parallel avatar or digital twin in cyberspace, such that we can conduct numerous scientific games before any major decision or operation. This new, yet unknown CPSS-enabled connected lifestyle and working environment will eventually lead to high satisfaction as well as enhanced capacity and efficiency. Further, the author of [52] foresees that the Multiverse or parallel universes based on Hugh Everett's many-worlds interpretation (MWI) of quantum physics will become a reality in the age of complex space infrastructures with the emergence of intelligent industries, which calls for a new profession of scientific game engineers. However, he warns that the capability of CPSS to collect tremendous energy from the masses through crowdsourcing in cyberspace and then release it into physical space can bring both favorable and unfavorable consequences. Therefore, one of the critical research challenges is the human-centric construction of complex spaces based on CPSS.

Similar to Industry 4.0/5.0, Society 5.0 merges the physical space and cyberspace by leveraging ICT to its fullest and applying not only social robots and embodied AI but also emerging technologies such as ambient intelligence, VR/AR, and advanced human–computer interfaces (HCIs). However, Society 5.0 counterbalances the commercial emphasis of Industry 4.0. If the Industry 4.0 paradigm is understood as focusing on the creation of the smart factory, Society 5.0 is geared toward creating the world's first supersmart society. More interestingly, according to Hitachi-UTokyo Laboratory [22], Society 5.0 also envisions a paradigm shift from conventional monetary to future non-monetary economies based on technologies that can measure activities toward human co-becoming that have no monetary value.

The relationship between Society 5.0 and past societies on the one hand and Industry 4.0 on the other hand was described in more detail in Hitachi-UTokyo Laboratory, 2020 [22]. While the focus of Society 4.0 was on building an information society via ICT for the purpose of increasing profitability, Society 5.0's main goal is to merge cyberspace and physical space for the purpose of advancing humanity. Society 5.0 seeks to revolutionize not only the industry through ICT but also the living spaces and habits of the public. Society 5.0 focuses heavily on the public impact of technology and aspires to create a supersmart society, thus requiring metrics that are much more complex than those used in Industry 4.0, whose focus centers on minimizing manufacturing costs without taking social issues into account.

Similar to Industry 4.0, Society 5.0 aims at seamlessly fusing the digital and physical worlds by using social robots, ambient intelligence, advanced HCI, embodied AI, and various flavors of extended reality including VR/AR, in addition to the aforementioned CPSS. Society 5.0 has two specific visions. The first one is human-robot co-working. In this vision, robots (including social robots) and humans will work together whenever and wherever possible. Humans will focus on tasks requiring creativity and robots will do the rest, giving rise to the aforementioned concept of the DAO. DAO is a unique feature of Ethereum blockchain and heavily relies on crowdsourcing human skills to solve problems that robots and autonomous AI agents alone cannot solve well. The second vision of Society 5.0 is bionics, which studies the smart use of biological resources for industrial purposes to help achieve a balance between society, economy, and ecology.

PURPOSE AND OUTLINE OF BOOK

The remainder of this book is structured as follows.

Chapter 2 investigates blockchain technologies with respect to its capability to develop new models of distributed ownership such as the Tactile Internet. In this chapter, we also discuss the similarities and differences between Bitcoin and Ethereum blockchains. The comparison determines that Ethereum is a better choice as a blockchain platform. We also argue that Ethereum is better than other blockchains because of a number of salient features including DAO and its cooperative working with AI and robots and also that it is highly compatible with decentralized edge computing solutions. In our studies, we show that DAO gives birth to a new hybrid form of collaboration, in which intelligence and automation are at the center and humans operate at the edges. Finally, we conclude the chapter by outlining open research challenges and future work.

Chapter 3 elaborates on the potential of the DAO to help decentralize the Tactile Internet as a future 6G application and aligns its decentralization with AI-enhanced multi-access edge computing (MEC). Our presented results demonstrate that higher degrees of decentralization lower the completion times of computational jobs. In addition, we extend the existent BIoT framework's judge contract, which controls IoT devices' behavior and punishes them by blocking network access, to a broader Tactile Internet context. The developed nudge contract aims at completing interrupted physical tasks by learning from a remote skilled human member of the DAO while minimizing the learning loss. Our nudge contract modifies human behavior by means of a suitable reward mechanism (instead of punishment) in order to foster trusted skill transfers.

Chapter 4 investigates the widely studied trust game of behavioral economics in a blockchain context, paying close attention to the importance of developing efficient cooperation and coordination techniques. After identifying open research challenges of blockchain-enabled implementations of the trust game, we first develop a smart contract that replaces the experimenter in the middle between trustor and trustee and demonstrates experimentally that a social efficiency of up to 100 percent can be achieved by using deposits to enhance both trust and trustworthiness. We then present an on-chaining blockchain oracle architecture for a networked N-player trust game that involves a third type of human agent called observers, who track the players' investment and reciprocity. The presence of third-party reward and penalty decisions helps raise the average normalized reciprocity above 80 percent, even without requiring any deposit. Further, we focus on the emerging field of robonomics in the 6G era, which studies the socio-technical impact of blockchain technologies on social human-robot interaction and behavioral economics for the social integration of robots into human society. Finally, we experimentally demonstrate that mixed logical-affective persuasive strategies for social robots improve the trustees' trustworthiness and reciprocity significantly.

Chapter 5 explores future 6G mobile networks and their anticipated shift to become more human-centered, thereby enabling the so-called Society 5.0 vision. Further, we build on our recent work on robonomics in the 6G era. As mentioned above, robonomics investigates social human-robot interaction and its socio-technical impact as well as blockchain technologies and cryptocurrencies, not only coins but—more interestingly—also tokens. Specifically, we study the tokenization process of creating tokenized digital twins of assets and access rights in the physical and digital world, paying close attention to its central role in the future Web3 and its underlying token economy, the successor of today's information and platform economies. After introducing our CPSS-based bottom-up multilayer token engineering framework for Society 5.0, we experimentally demonstrate how the collective human intelligence of a blockchain-enabled DAO can be enhanced via purpose-driven tokens.

Finally, Chapter 6 concludes the book by summarizing the major findings of the book.

NOTES

1. International Telecommunication Union—Telecommunication Standardization Sector (ITU-T)
2. MakerDAO white paper: https://makerdao.com/en/whitepaper/
3. https://aragon.org/
4. https://alchemy.daostack.io/
5. https://colony.io/
6. Colony Technical White Paper, https://colony.io/whitepaper.pdf
7. https://github.com/orisi/orisi
8. https://provable.xyz/
9. https://chain.link/
10. https://eips.ethereum.org/EIPS/eip-20
11. https://eips.ethereum.org/EIPS/eip-721
12. https://www.cryptovoxels.com/parcels/2
13. https://eips.ethereum.org/EIPS/eip-1155

REFERENCES

1. C. Rowell and S. Han, "Practical Large Scale Antenna Systems for 5G Cellular Networks," in *Proceedings of IEEE International Wireless Symposium (IWS 2015)*, pp. 1–4, July 2015.
2. P. Semov, P. Koleva, K. Tonchev, V. Poulkov and T. Cooklev, "Evolution of Mobile Networks and C-RAN on the Road Beyond 5G," *International Conference on Telecommunications and Signal Processing (TSP)*, pp. 392–398, July 2020.

3. P. Rost, A. Banchs, I. Berberana, M. Breitbach, M. Doll, H. Droste, C. Mannweiler, M. A. Puente, K. Samdanis, B. Sayadi, "Mobile Network Architecture Evolution toward 5G," *IEEE Communications Magazine,* vol. 54, no. 5, pp. 84–91, May 2016.

4. R. Askar, J. Chung, Z. Guo, H. Ko, W. Keusgen and T. Haustein, "Interference Handling Challenges toward Full Duplex Evolution in 5G and Beyond Cellular Networks," *IEEE Wireless Communications,* vol. 28, no. 1, pp. 51–59, February 2021.

5. K. Samdanis and T. Taleb, "The Road beyond 5G: A Vision and Insight of the Key Technologies," *IEEE Network,* vol. 34, no. 2, pp. 135–141, March/April 2020.

6. G. P. Fettweis, "The Tactile Internet: Applications and Challenges," *IEEE Vehicular Technology Magazine,* vol. 9, no. 1, pp. 64–70, March 2014.

7. M. Simsek, A. Aijaz, M. Dohler, J. Sachs and G. Fettweis, "5G-Enabled Tactile Internet," *IEEE Journal on Selected Areas in Communications,* vol. 34, no. 3, pp. 460–473, March 2016.

8. M. Maier, M. Chowdhury, B. P. Rimal and D. P. Van, "The Tactile Internet: Vision, Recent Progress, and Open Challenges," *IEEE Communications Magazine,* vol. 54, no. 5, pp. 138–145, May 2016.

9. M. Dohler, T. Mahmoodi, M. A. Lema, M. Condoluci, F. Sardis, K. Antonakoglou and H. Aghvami, "Internet of Skills, Where Robotics Meets AI, 5G and the Tactile Internet," in *Proceedings of European Conference on Networks and Communications (EuCNC),* Oulu, June 2017, pp. 1–5.

10. M. Dohler, "The Future and Challenges of Communications—Toward a World Where 5G Enables Synchronized Reality and an Internet of Skills," *Internet Technology Letters,* vol. 1, no. 2, pp. 1–3, April 2018.

11. M. A. Lema, A. Laya, T. Mahmoodi, M. Cuevas, J. Sachs, J. Markendahl and M. Dohler, "Business Case and Technology Analysis for 5G Low Latency Applications," *IEEE Access,* vol. 5, pp. 5917–5935, April 2017.

12. ITU-T, "The Tactile Internet," *International Telecommunication Union (ITU),* Technology Watch Report, August 2014.

13. M. Maier, A. Ebrahimzadeh, S. Rostami and A. Beniiche, "The Internet of No Things: Making the Internet Disappear and 'See the Invisible,'" *IEEE Communications Magazine,* vol. 58, no. 11, pp. 76–82, November 2020.

14. G. Dublon and J. A. Paradiso, "Extra Sensory Perception," *Scientific American,* vol. 311, no. 1, pp. 36–41, July 2014.

15. M. Weiser, "The Computer for the 21st Century," *Scientific American,* vol. 265, no. 3, pp. 94–104, September 1991.

16. M. Maier and A. Ebrahimzadeh, "Towards Immersive Tactile Internet Experiences: Low-Latency FiWi Enhanced Mobile Networks with Edge Intelligence [Invited]," *IEEE/OSA Journal of Optical Communications and Networking, Special Issue on Latency in Edge Optical Networks,* vol. 11, no. 4, pp. B10–B25, April 2019.

17. T. Huang, W. Yang, J. Wu, J. Ma, X. Zhang and D. Zhang, "A Survey on Green 6G Network: Architecture and Technologies," *IEEE Access,* vol. 7, pp. 175758–175768, December 2019.

18. G. Liu et al., "Vision, Requirements and Network Architecture of 6G Mobile Network beyond 2030," in *China Communications,* vol. 17, no. 9, pp. 92–104, September 2020.

19. M. Giordani, M. Polese, M. Mezzavilla, S. Rangan and M. Zorzi, "Toward 6G Networks: Use Cases and Technologies," *IEEE Communications Magazine*, vol. 58, no. 3, pp. 55–61, March 2020.

20. Q. Bi, "Ten Trends in the Cellular Industry and an Outlook on 6G," *IEEE Communications Magazine*, vol. 57, pp. 31–36, December 2019.

21. M. Latva-aho and K. Leppänen (eds.), "6G White Paper, Key Drivers and Research Challenges for 6G Ubiquitous Wireless Intelligence," September 2019.

22. Hitachi-UTokyo Laboratory (H-UTokyo Lab), "*Society 5.0: A People-Centric Super-Smart Society*," *Springer Open*, Singapore, 2020.

23. S. Zhang, C. Xiang and S. Xu, "6G: Connecting Everything by 1000 Times Price Reduction," *IEEE Open Journal of Vehicular Technology*, vol. 1, pp. 107–115, March 2020.

24. E. Yaacoub and M. Alouini, "A Key 6G Challenge and Opportunity—Connecting the Base of the Pyramid: A Survey on Rural Connectivity [Invited Paper]," *Proceedings of the IEEE*. vol. 108, no. 4, pp. 533–582, April 2020.

25. S. Nakamoto, "Bitcoin: A Peer-to-Peer Electronic Cash System," *Decentralized Business Review*, p. 21260, 2008.

26. Y. Hu, H. G. A. Valera and L. Oxley, "Market Efficiency of the Top Market-Cap Cryptocurrencies: Further Evidence from a Panel Framework," *Finance Research Letters*, vol. 31, issue C, pp. 138–145, 2019.

27. F. Tschorsch and B. Scheuermann, "Bitcoin and Beyond: A Technical Survey on Decentralized Digital Currencies," *IEEE Communications Surveys & Tutorials*, vol. 18, no. 3, pp. 2084–2123, Third Quarter 2016.

28. R. Beck, "Beyond Bitcoin: The Rise of Blockchain World," *IEEE Computer*, vol. 51, no. 2, pp. 54–58, Feb. 2018.

29. D. Tapscott and A. Tapscott, "Blockchain Revolution: How the Technology Behind Bitcoin Is Changing Money, Business, and the World," Portfolio, Toronto, May 2016.

30. W. Yang, S. Garg, A. Raza, D. Herbert and B. Kang, "Blockchain: Trends and future," *In Pacific Rim Knowledge Acquisition Workshop*, Springer, Cham, pp. 201–210, August 2018.

31. V. Buterin, "A Next-Generation Smart Contract and Decentralized Application Platform," Ethereum White Paper, https://www.ethereum.org.

32. S. Junichi and K. Yasuhiro, "Blockchain 3.0: Internet of Value—Human Technology for the Realization of a Society Where the Existence of Exceptional Value is Allowed," *Human Interaction, Emerging Technologies and Future Applications IV*, Springer International, Cham, pp. 569–577, April 2021.

33. L. Seok-Won, I. Singh and M. Mohammadian, (eds), "*Blockchain Technology for IoT Applications,*" *Springer Nature*, 2021.

34. S. Voshmgir, "*Token Economy: How the Web3 reinvents the Internet (Second Edition),*" BlockchainHub, Berlin, June 2020.

35. G. Caldarelli, "Real-World Blockchain Applications Under the Lens of the Oracle Problem. A Systematic Literature Review," *IEEE International Conference on Technology Management, Operations and Decisions (ICTMOD)*, Marrakech, pp. 1–6, November 2020.

36. H. Al-Breiki, M. H. U. Rehman, K. Salah and D. Svetinovic, "Trustworthy Blockchain Oracles: Review, Comparison, and Open Research Challenges," *IEEE Access*, vol. 8, pp. 85675–85685, May 2020.

37. S. Tikhomirov, E. Voskresenskaya, I. Ivanitskiy, R. Takhaviev, E. Marchenko and Y. Alexandrov, "Smartcheck: Static Analysis Of Ethereum Smart Contracts," In *Proceedings of the 1st International Workshop on Emerging Trends in Software Engineering for Blockchain (WET- SEB '18)*, ACM, New York, NYA, pp. 9–16. May 2018.

38. Y. Faqir-Rhazoui, J. Arroyo and S. Hassa, "A Scalable Voting System: Validation of Holographic Consensus in DAOstack," In *Proceedings of the 54th Hawaii International Conference on System Sciences*, p. 5557, Jan. 2021.

39. J. Wolfers and E. Zitzewitz, "Prediction markets," *Journal of Economic Perspectives*, vol. 18, no. 2, pp. 107–126, 2004.

40. M. Mannan, "Fostering Worker Cooperatives with Blockchain Technology: Lessons from the Colony Project," *Erasmus Law Review*, vol. 11, p. 190, 2018.

41. M. Merlini, N. Veira, R. Berryhill and A. Veneris, "On Public Decentralized Ledger Oracles via a Paired-Question Protocol," *IEEE International Conference on Blockchain and Cryptocurrency (ICBC), Seoul*, pp. 337–344, May 2019.

42. N. Neidhardt, C. Köhler and M. Nüttgens, "Cloud Service Billing and Service Level Agreement Monitoring based on Blockchain," In *EMISA. CEUR Workshop Proceedings*, vol. 2097, pp. 65–69, 2018.

43. A. S. de Pedro Crespo, D. Levi, L. I. C. García, "Witnet: A Decentralized Oracle Network Protocol," 2017.

44. X. Xu, C. Pautasso, L. Zhu, V. Gramoli, A. Ponomarev, A.B. Tran, S. Chen, "The Blockchain as a Software Connector," *13th Working IEEE/IFIP Conference on Software Architecture (WICSA)*, Venice, pp. 182–191, July 2016.

45. J. Adler, R. Berryhill, A. Veneris, Z. Poulos, N. Veira and A. Kastania, "ASTRAEA: A Decentralized Blockchain Oracle," *Proceedings of IEEE International Conference on Cyber, Physical and Social Computing*, Halifax, NS, Canada, pp. 1145–1152, July/August 2018.

46. F. Zhang, E. Cecchetti, K. Croman, A. Juels and E. Shi, "Town Crier: An Authenticated Data Feed for Smart Contracts," In *Proceedings of the 2016 ACM SIGSAC Conference on Computer and Communications Security (CCS '16)*, ACM, New York, NY, USA, pp. 270–282, October 2016.

47. J. Heiss, J. Eberhardt and S. Tai, "From Oracles to Trustworthy Data Onchaining Systems," *Proceedings of IEEE International Conference on Blockchain*, Atlanta, GA, USA, pp. 496–503, July 2019.

48. J. Cotta, M. Breque, L. De Nul and A. Petridis, "Industry 5.0: Towards more Sustainable, Human-Centric and Resilient Industry," European Commission Research and Innovation (R&I) Series Policy Brief, January 2021.

49. Y. Zhou, F. R. Yu, J. Chen and Y. Kuo, "Cyber-Physical-Social Systems: A State-of-the-Art Survey, Challenges and Opportunities," *IEEE Communications Surveys & Tutorials*, vol. 22, no. 1, pp. 389–425, First quarter 2020.

50. K. A. Demir, G. Döven and B. Sezen, "Industry 5.0 and Human-Robot o-working," *Procedia Computer Science*, vol. 158, pp. 688–695, 2019.

51. G. Schütte, "What Kind of Innovation Policy Does the Bioeconomy Need?" *New Biotechnology*, vol. 40, Part A, pp. 82–86, Jan. 2018.

52. F.-Y. Wang, "The Emergence of Intelligent Enterprises: From CPS to CPSS," *IEEE Intelligent Systems*, vol. 25, no. 4, pp. 85–88, July/Aug. 2010.

Blockchain, AI, and Human Intelligence

2

The Path toward 6G

INTRODUCTION

The Internet has been constantly evolving from the mobile Internet to the emerging Internet of Things (IoT) and future Tactile Internet. Similarly, the capabilities of future 5G networks will extend far beyond those of previous generations of mobile communication. Besides 1000-fold gains in area capacity, 10 Gb/s peak data rates, and connections for at least 100 billion devices, an important aspect of the 5G vision is *decentralization*. While 2G, 3G, and 4G cellular networks were built under the design premise of having complete control at the infrastructure side, 5G systems may drop this design assumption and evolve the cell-centric architecture into a more device-centric one. Although there is a significant overlap of design objectives among 5G, IoT, and the Tactile Internet—most notably, ultra-reliable and low-latency communication (URLLC)—each one of them exhibits unique characteristics in terms of underlying communications paradigms and enabling end devices [1]. Today's Internet is ushering in a new era. While the first generation of digital revolution brought us the Internet of information, the second generation—powered by decentralized blockchain technology—is bringing us the Internet of value, a true peer-to-peer (P2P) platform that has the potential to go far beyond digital currencies and record virtually everything of value to humankind in a distributed fashion without powerful intermediaries [2]. Some refer to decentralized blockchain technology as the "alchemy of the 21st century" because it may leverage end-user equipment for converting computing into

DOI: 10.1201/9781003427322-2

digital gold. More importantly, though, according to Don and Alex Tapscott, the blockchain technology enables trusted collaboration that can start to change the way wealth is distributed because people can share more fully in the wealth they create, rather than trying to solve the problem of growing social inequality through the redistribution of wealth only. As a result, decentralized blockchain technology helps create platforms for distributed capitalism and a more inclusive economy, which works best when it works for everyone as the foundation for prosperity. Furthermore, Saad et al. [3] pointed out the important role of blockchain and distributed ledger technology (DLT) applications as a next generation of distributed sensing services for 6G-driving applications whose need for connectivity will require a synergistic mix of URLLC and massive machine-type communications (mMTC) to guarantee low latency, reliable connectivity, and scalability. Furthermore, blockchains and smart contracts can improve the security of a wide range of businesses by ensuring that data cannot be damaged, stolen, or lost. Salman et al. [4] presented a comprehensive survey on the use of blockchain technologies to provide distributed security services. These services include entity authentication, confidentiality, privacy, provenance, and integrity assurances.

A blockchain technology of particular interest is Ethereum, which went live in July 2015. Ethereum was founded by Canadian Vitalik Buterin after his request for creating a wider and more general scripting language for the development of decentralized applications (DApps) that are not limited to cryptocurrencies, a capability that Bitcoin lacked, was rejected by the Bitcoin community [5]. Ethereum enables new forms of economic organization and distributed models of companies, businesses, and ownership (e.g., self-organized holarchies and member-owned cooperatives). Or as Buterin puts it, while most technologies tend to automate workers on the periphery doing menial tasks, Ethereum automates away the center. For instance, instead of putting the taxi driver out of a job, Ethereum puts Uber out of a job and lets the taxi drivers work with the customer directly (before Uber's self-driving cars will eventually wipe out their jobs). Hence, Ethereum does not aim at eliminating jobs, so much as it changes the definition of work. In fact, it gave rise to the first decentralized autonomous organization (DAO) built within the Ethereum project. The DAO is an open-source, distributed software that exists "simultaneously nowhere and everywhere," thereby creating a paradigm shift that offers new opportunities to democratize business and enables entrepreneurs of the future to design their own virtual organizations customized to the optimal needs of their mission, vision, and strategy to change the world [6].

There exist excellent surveys on Bitcoin and other decentralized digital currencies (e.g., [7]). Likewise, the fundamental concepts and potential of blockchain technologies for society and industry in general have been described comprehensively in various existent tutorials (e.g., [8]). In this chapter, we focus on how blockchain technologies can be used in an IoT context by providing an up-to-date survey on recent progress and open challenges for realizing the emerging blockchain IoT (B-IoT). Unlike the IoT without any human involvement in its underlying machine-to-machine (M2M) communications, the Tactile Internet is anticipated to keep the human in (rather than out of) the loop by providing real-time transmission of haptic information, (i.e., touch and actuation) for the remote control of physical or virtual objects through the Internet. Toward this end, we elaborate on how Ethereum blockchain technologies, in particular the DAO, may be leveraged to realize future techno-social systems, notably the Tactile Internet, which is yet unclear in how exactly it would work [8].

The remainder of this chapter is structured as follows. In "Ethereum versus Bitcoin Blockchains" section, we first explain the commonalities of and specific differences between Ethereum and Bitcoin blockchains in greater detail. "Blockchain IoT (B-IoT): Recent Progress and Related Work" section then reviews recent progress and open challenges of the emerging B-IoT. In "The IEEE P1918.1 Tactile Internet" section, after briefly reviewing the key concepts of the emerging Tactile Internet, we introduce the so-called human-agent-robot teamwork (HART) design approach and our proposed low-latency FiWi enhanced LTE-A HetNets based on advanced multi-access edge computing with embedded artificial intelligence (AI) capabilities. In "Decentralizing the Tactile Internet" section, we elaborate on the potential role of Ethereum and, in particular the DAO, in helping decentralize the Tactile Internet. "Blockchain, AI, and Human Intelligence: The Path Forward" section discusses the symbiosis of blockchain, AI, and augmented intelligence in more detail, and "Open Challenges and Future Work" section suggests future research areas. Finally, "Conclusions" section concludes the chapter.

BLOCKCHAIN TECHNOLOGIES

In this section, we give a brief overview of the basic concepts of blockchain technologies, paying particular attention to the main commonalities and specific differences between Ethereum and Bitcoin. We then introduce the DAO, which represents a salient feature of Ethereum that cannot be found in Bitcoin.

Ethereum versus Bitcoin Blockchains

Blockchain technologies have been undergoing several iterations as both public organizations and private corporations seek to take advantage of their potential. A typical blockchain network is essentially a distributed database (also known as a "ledger"), comprising records of all transactions or digital events that have been executed by or shared among participating parties. Blockchains may be categorized into public (i.e., permissionless) and private (i.e., permissioned) networks. In the former category, anyone may join and participate in the blockchain. Conversely, a private blockchain applies certain access control mechanisms to determine who can join the network. A public blockchain is immutable because none of the transactions can be tampered with or changed. Also, it is pseudo-anonymous because the identity of those involved in a transaction is represented by an address key in the form of a random string. Table 2.1 highlights the major differences between public and private blockchains, as will be discussed in further detail. Note that both Ethereum and Bitcoin are public blockchains. Figure 2.1 illustrates the main commonalities and differences between Bitcoin and Ethereum blockchains. The Bitcoin blockchain is predominantly designed to facilitate Bitcoin transactions. It is the world's first fully functional digital currency that is truly decentralized, open source, and censorship resistant. Bitcoin makes use of a cryptographic proof-of-work (PoW) consensus mechanism based on the SHA-256 hash function and digital signatures. Achieving consensus provides extreme levels of fault tolerance, ensures zero downtime, and makes data stored on the blockchain forever unchangeable and censorship-resistant in

TABLE 2.1   Public versus private blockchains

	PUBLIC BLOCKCHAIN	PRIVATE BLOCKCHAIN
Network Type	Fully decentralized	Partially decentralized
Access	Permissionless read/write	Permissioned read/write
User Identity	Pseudo-anonymous	Known participants
Consensus Mechanism	Proof-of-work/ Proof-of-state	Pre-approved participants
Consensus Determination	By all miners	By one organization
Immutability	Nearly impossible to tamper	Could be tampered
Purpose	Any decentralized applications	Business applications

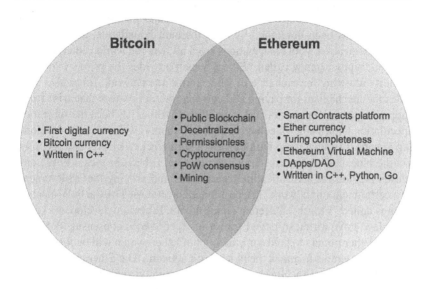

Bitcoin

Ethereum

- First digital currency
- Bitcoin currency
- Written in C++

- Public Blockchain
- Decentralized
- Permissionless
- Cryptocurrency
- PoW consensus
- Mining

- Smart Contracts platform
- Ether currency
- Turing completeness
- Ethereum Virtual Machine
- DApps/DAO
- Written in C++, Python, Go

FIGURE 2.1   Bitcoin and Ethereum blockchains: Commonalities and differences.

that everyone can see the blockchain history, including any data or messages. There are two different types of actors, whose roles are defined as follows:

- *Regular nodes*: A regular node is a conventional actor, who just has a copy of the blockchain and uses the blockchain network to send or receive Bitcoins.
- *Miners*: A miner is an actor with a particular role, who builds the blockchain through the validation of transactions by creating blocks and submitting them to the blockchain network to be included as blocks. Miners serve as protectors of the network and can operate from anywhere in the world as long as they have sufficient knowledge about the mining process, the hardware and software required to do so, and an Internet connection.

In the Bitcoin blockchain, a block is mined about every 10 minutes, and the block size is limited to 1 MByte. Note that the Bitcoin blockchain is restricted to a rate of seven transactions per second, which renders it unsuitable for high-frequency trading. Other weaknesses of the Bitcoin blockchain include its script language, which offers only a limited number of small instructions and is non-Turing-complete. Furthermore, developing applications using the Bitcoin script language requires advanced skills in programming and cryptography.

Ethereum is currently the second-most popular public blockchain after Bitcoin. It has been developed by the Ethereum Foundation, a Swiss non-profit organization, with contributions from all over the world. Ethereum has its own cryptocurrency called "Ether," which provides the primary form of liquidity allowing for exchange of value across the network. Ether also provides the mechanism for paying and earning transaction fees that arise from supporting and using the network. Like Bitcoin, Ether has been the subject of speculation witnessing wide fluctuations. Ethereum is well suited for developing DApps that need to be built quickly and interact efficiently and securely via the blockchain platform. Similar to Bitcoin, Ethereum uses a PoW consensus method for authenticating transactions and proving the achievement of a certain amount of work. The hashing algorithm used by the PoW mechanism is called "Ethash." Different from Bitcoin, Ethereum developers expect to replace PoW with a so-called "proof-of-stake" (PoS) consensus. PoS will require Ether miners to hold some amount of Ether, which will be forfeited if the miner attempts to attack the blockchain network. The Ethereum platform is often referred to as a "Turing-complete Ethereum virtual machine (EVM)" built on top of the underlying blockchain. Turing-completeness means that any system or programming language is able to compute anything computable, provided it has enough resources. Note that the EVM requires a small amount of fee for executing transactions. These fees are called "gas," and the required amount of gas depends on the size of a given instruction. The longer the instruction, the more gas is required.

Whereas the Bitcoin blockchain simply contains a list of transactions, Ethereum's basic unit is the "account." The Ethereum blockchain tracks the state of every account, whereby all state transitions are transfers of value and information between accounts. The account concept is considered an essential component and data model of the Ethereum blockchain because it is vital for a user to interact with the Ethereum network via transactions. Accounts represent the identities of external agents (e.g., human or automated agents, mining nodes). Accounts use public key cryptography to sign each transaction such that the EVM can securely validate the identity of the sender of the transaction.

Beside C++, Ethereum supports several programming languages based on JavaScript and Python (e.g., Solidity, Serpent, Mutan, or LLL), whereby Solidity is the most popular language for writing so-called 'smart contracts. A smart contract is an agreement that runs exactly as programmed without any third-party interference. It uses its own arbitrary rules of ownership, transaction formats, and state-transition logic. Each method of a smart contract can be invoked via either a transaction or another method. Smart contracts enable the realization of DApps, which may look exactly the same as conventional applications with regard to application programming interface (API), though the centralized backend services are replaced with smart contracts running on the decentralized Ethereum network without relying on any central servers. Interesting examples of existent DApps include Augur (a decentralized prediction market), Weifund (an open platform for crowdfunding), Golem (supercomputing), and Ethlance (decentralized job market platform), among others. To provide an effective means of communications between DApps, Ethereum uses the Whisper P2P protocol, a fully decentralized middleware for secret messaging and digital cryptography. Whisper supports the creation of confidential communication routes without the need for a trusted third party. It builds on a peer sampling service that takes into account network limitations such as network address translation (NAT) and firewalls. In general, any centralized service may be converted into a DApp by using the Ethereum blockchain.

Decentralized Autonomous Organizations (DAOs)

The most remarkable thing about cryptocurrencies and blockchain might be how they enable people and organizations on a global level, all acting in their own interest, to create something of immense shared value. Many observers assert that this is a real alternative to current companies. The decentralization, crowd-based technologies of cryptocurrencies, distributed ledgers, distributed consensus, and smart contracts provide the possibility to fundamentally change the way people organize their affairs and offer a new paradigm for enterprise design. Two recent efforts to substitute a crowd for a company are blockchain technology and DAOs. DAOs are decentralized organizations without a central authority or leader. They operate on a programming code that is encoded on the Ethereum blockchain. Like the blockchain, the code of a DAO moves away from traditional organizations by removing the need for centralized control. Not even the original developers of the DAO have any extra authority because it runs independently without any human intervention. It may be funded by a group of individuals who cover its basic costs and give the funders voting rights rather than any kind of ownership or equity shares. This creates an autonomous and transparent system that will continue on the network for as long as it provides a useful service to its customers.

A successful example of deploying the DAO concept for automated smart contract operation is Storj, which is a decentralized, secure, private, and encrypted cloud storage platform that may be used as an alternative to centralized storage providers like Dropbox or Google Drive. A DAO may be funded by a group of individuals who cover its basic costs, giving the funders voting rights rather than any kind of ownership or equity shares. This creates an autonomous and transparent system that will continue on the network for as long as it provides a useful service for its customers. DAOs exist as open-source, distributed software that executes smart contracts and works according to specified governance rules and guidelines. Buterin described the ideal of a DAO on the Ethereum Blog as follows: "It is an entity that lives on the Internet and exists autonomously, but also heavily relies on hiring individuals to perform certain tasks that the automation itself cannot do." Unlike AI-based agents that are completely autonomous, a DAO still requires heavy involvement from humans specifically interacting according to a protocol defined by the DAO to operate. For illustrating the distinction between a DAO and AI, Fig. 2.2 shows a quadrant chart that classifies DAOs, AI, traditional organizations as well as robots, which have been widely deployed in assembly lines among others, with regard to automation and humans involved at their edges and center. We will elaborate on how this particular feature of DAOs (i.e., automation at the center and humans at the edges) can be exploited for decentralizing the Tactile Internet in "Decentralizing the Tactile Internet" section. Toward this end, we also briefly note that according to Buterin a DAO is non-profit, though one can make money in a DAO, not by providing investment into the DAO itself but by participating in its ecosystem (e.g., via membership).

For convenience, Table 2.2 summarizes the technical details of our comparison of Bitcoin and Ethereum blockchains.

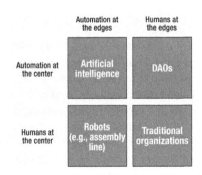

FIGURE 2.2 DAOs versus artificial intelligence, traditional organizations, and robots (widely deployed in assembly lines, among others): Automation and humans involved at their edges and center. (From Ethereum blog.)

TABLE 2.2   Comparison of Bitcoin and Ethereum blockchains

	BITCOIN	ETHEREUM
Currency	Bitcoin	Ether
Applications	Cryptocurrency	Cryptocurrency, Smart Contract, DApps/DAO
Written in	C++	C++, Go, Python
Consensus	Proof-of-work (based on SHA-256)	Proof-of-work (Ethash), Planning for proof-of-stake
Turing Completeness	No	Yes
Anonymity Mechanisms	No	Yes (with Whisper protocol)
Censorship Resistance	No	Yes
Transaction Limit	7 transactions/sec	20 transactions/sec
State Concept	No	Data
Smart Contract Languages	No	Solidity, Serpent, Mutan, LLL
Smart Contract Execution	No	Ethereum Virtual Machine (EVM)
Block Time	10 minutes	15 seconds
Data Model	Transaction-based	Account-based
Client P2P Connections	No	Yes (with Whisper protocol)
Routing	No	Yes (Whisper protocol)

BLOCKCHAIN IoT AND EDGE COMPUTING

In this section, after defining the integration of blockchain and IoT (B-IoT), we discuss the motivation for such integration followed by a description of the challenges of integrating blockchain and edge computing.

Blockchain IoT (B-IoT): Recent Progress and Related Work

Recall from Introduction that the IoT is designed to enable communications among machines without relying on any human involvement. Thus, its underlying M2M communications is useful for enabling the automation of industrial and other machine-centric processes. The emerging B-IoT represents a powerful combination of two massive technologies—blockchain and M2M communications—that allows us to automate complex multistep IoT processes (e.g., via smart contracts). With the ever-increasing variety of communication protocols between IoT devices, there is a need for transparent yet highly secure and reliable IoT device management systems. This section surveys the state of the art of the emerging B-IoT, describing recent progress and open challenges.

The majority of IoT devices are resource constrained, which restricts them to be part of the blockchain network. To cope with these limitations, Novo [9] proposed a decentralized access management system, where all entities are part of an Ethereum blockchain except for IoT devices as well as so-called "management hub" nodes that request permissions from the blockchain on behalf of the IoT devices belonging to different wireless sensor networks. In addition, entities called "managers" interact with the smart contract hosted at a specific "agent node" in the blockchain to define or modify the access control policies for the resources of their associated IoT devices. The proof-of-concept implementation evaluated the new system architecture components that are not part of the Ethereum network (i.e., management hub and IoT devices) and demonstrated the feasibility of the proposed access management architecture in terms of latency and scalability. Another interesting Ethereum case study can be found in [10], which reviews readily available Ethereum blockchain packages for realizing a smart home system according to its smart contract features for handling access control policy, data storage, and data flow management.

The architectural issues for realizing blockchain-driven IoT services were investigated in greater detail by Liao et al. [11]. In a preliminary study using a smart-thing-renting service as an example B-IoT service, the authors compared the following four different architectural styles based on Ethereum: (i) fully centralized (cloud without blockchain), (ii) pseudo-distributed things (physically located in central cloud), (iii) distributed things (directly controlled by smart contract), and (iv) fully distributed. The preliminary results indicate that a fully distributed architecture, where a blockchain endpoint is deployed on the end-user device, is superior in terms of robustness and security.

The various perspectives for integrating secure elements in Ethereum transactions were discussed in [12]. A novel architecture for establishing trust in Ethereum transactions exchanged by smart things was presented. To prevent the risks that secret keys for signature are stolen or hacked, the author proposed to use javacard-secure elements and a so-called "cryptocurrency smart card" (CCSC). Two CCSC use cases were discussed. In the first one, the CCSC was integrated in a low-cost B-IoT device powered by an Arduino processor, in which sensor data are integrated in Ethereum transactions. The second use case involved the deployment of CCSC in remote APDU call secure (RACS) servers to enable remote and safe digital signatures by using the well-known elliptic curve digital signature algorithm (ECDSA).

Blockchain transactions require public-key encryption operations such as digital signatures. However, not all B-IoT devices can support this computationally intensive task. For this reason, Polyzos and Fotiou [13] proposed a preliminary design of a gateway-oriented approach, where all blockchain-related operations are offloaded to a gateway. The authors noted that their approach is compatible with the Ethereum client-side architecture.

Because of the massive scale and distributed nature of IoT applications and services, blockchain technology can be exploited to provide a secure, tamper-proof B-IoT network. More specifically, the key properties of tamper-resistance and decentralized trust allow us to build a secure authentication and authorization service, which does not have a single point of failure. Toward this end, Gupta et al. [14] made a preliminary attempt to develop a security model backed by blockchain that provides confidentiality, integrity, and availability of data transmitted and received by nodes in a B-IoT network. The proposed solution encompasses a blockchain protocol layer on top of the TCP/IP transport layer and a blockchain application layer. The first one comprises a distributed consensus algorithm for B-IoT nodes, whereas the latter one defines the IoT security-specific transactions and their semantics for the higher protocol layers. To evaluate the feasibility and performance of the proposed layered architecture, B-IoT nodes connected in a tree topology were simulated using 1 Gbps Ethernet or 54 Mbps WiFi links. The simulation results showed that the block arrival rate was not affected much by the increased latency and reduced bandwidth when replacing wired Ethernet with wireless WiFi links because the block difficulty adjustment adapts dynamically to the network conditions.

Among various low-power wide-area (LPWA) technologies, long-range (LoRa) wireless radio frequency (RF) is considered one of the most promising enabling technologies for realizing massive IoT deployment. Özyilmaz and Yurdakul [15] presented a proof-of-concept demonstrator to enable low-power, resource-constrained LoRa IoT end devices to access an Ethereum blockchain network via an intermediate gateway, which acts as a full blockchain node. More specifically, a battery-powered IoT end device sends position data to the LoRa gateway, which in turn forwards it through the standard Go-lang-based Ethereum client Geth to the blockchain network using a smart contract. An event-based communication mechanism between the LoRa gateway and a backend application server was implemented as proof-of-concept demonstrator.

One of the fundamental challenges of object identification in IoT stems from the traditional domain name system (DNS). Typically, DNS is managed in centralized modules and, thus, may cause large-scale failures as a result of unilateral advanced persistent threat (APT) attacks as well as zone file synchronization delays in larger systems. Clearly, a more robust and distributed name management system is needed that supports the smooth evolution of DNS and renders it more efficient for IoT and the future Internet in general. Toward this end, a decentralized blockchain-based domain name system called "DNSLedger" was introduced by Duan et al. [16]. To rebuild the hierarchical structure of DNS, DNSLedger contains two kinds of blockchain: (i) a single root chain that stores all the top-level domain information and (ii) multiple top-level domain (TLD) chains, each responsible for the information about its respective domain name. In DNSLedger, servers of domain names act as blockchain nodes, while each TLD chain may select one or more servers to join the root chain. DNSLedger clients may execute common DNS functions such as domain name lookup, application, and modification.

Many of the aforementioned studies considered Ethereum as the blockchain of choice. It was shown that fully distributed Ethereum architectures are able to enhance both robustness and security. Furthermore, a gateway-oriented design approach was often applied to offload computationally intensive tasks from low-power, resource-constrained IoT end devices onto an intermediate gateway and, thus, enable them to access the Ethereum blockchain network. Also, it was shown that the block arrival rate does not deteriorate much by the increased latency and reduced bandwidth of WiFi access links.

Despite the recent progress, the salient features that set Ethereum aside from other blockchains (see "Ethereum versus Bitcoin Blockchains" section) remain to be explored in more depth, including their symbiosis with other emerging key technologies such as AI and robots as well as decentralized cloud computing solutions known as "edge computing."

A question of particular interest hereby is how decentralized blockchain mechanisms may be leveraged to let new hybrid forms of collaboration among individuals, which have not been entertained in the traditional market-oriented economy dominated by firms rather than individuals [8].

Blockchain-Enabled Edge Computing

One of the critical challenges in cloud computing is the end-to-end responsiveness between the mobile device and an associated cloud. To address this challenge, multi-access edge computing (MEC) is proposed, which is a mobility-enhanced small-scale cloud data center that is located at the edge of the Internet (e.g., Radio Access Network [RAN]) and in close proximity to mobile subscribers. An MEC entity is a trusted, resource-rich computer or cluster of computers that is well-connected to the Internet and available for use by nearby mobile devices. According to the white paper published by ETSI, MEC is considered a key emerging technology to be an important component of next-generation networks. In light of the aforementioned arguments, the integration of blockchain and edge computing into one unified entity becomes a natural trend. On one hand, by incorporating blockchain into the edge computing network, the system can provide reliable access and control of the network, computation, and storage over decentralized nodes. On the other hand, edge computing enables blockchain storage and mining computation from power-limited devices. Furthermore, off-chain storage and off-chain computation at the edges enable scalable storage and computation on the blockchain [17].

Several recent studies on blockchain and edge computing have been carried out. In [18], resource-constrained IoT devices were released from computation-intensive tasks by offloading blockchain consensus processes and data-processing tasks onto more powerful edge computing resources. The proposed EdgeChain was built on the Ethereum platform and uses smart contracts to monitor and regulate the behavior of IoT devices based on how they act and use resources. Another blockchain-enabled computation offloading scheme for IoT with edge computing capabilities, called "BeCome," was proposed in [19]. The authors of this study aimed at decreasing the task offloading time and energy consumption of edge computing devices, while achieving load balancing and data integrity.

The study by Zhaofeng et al. [20] proposed a blockchain-based trusted data management scheme called "BlockTDM" for edge computing to solve the data trust and security problems in an edge computing environment. Specifically, the authors proposed a flexible and configurable blockchain architecture that includes a mutual authentication protocol, flexible consensus, smart contract, block and transaction data management as well as blockchain node management and deployment. The BlockTDM scheme is able to support matrix-based multichannel data segment and isolation for sensitive or privacy data protection. Moreover, the authors designed user-defined sensitive data encryption before the transaction payload is stored in the blockchain system. They implemented a conditional access and decryption query of the protected blockchain data and transactions through an appropriate smart contract. Their analysis and evaluation show that the proposed BlockTDM scheme provides a general, flexible, and configurable blockchain-based paradigm for trusted data management with high credibility.

In summary, blockchain-enabled edge computing has become an important concept that leverages decentralized management and distributed services to meet the security, scalability, and performance requirements of next-generation of communications networks, as discussed in technically greater detail in "Decentralizing the Tactile Internet."

THE IEEE P1918.1 TACTILE INTERNET

In this section, we give a brief overview of the basic concepts, features, structure, and taxonomy of the Tactile Internet. Subsequently, some of the typical Tactile Internet applications and network infrastructure requirements are presented in greater detail.

The Tactile Internet: Key Principles

The term "Tactile Internet" was first coined by Fettweis in 2014. In his seminal paper [21], the Tactile Internet was defined as a breakthrough enabling unprecedented mobile applications for tactile steering and control of real and virtual objects by requiring a round-trip latency of 1–10 ms. Later in 2014, ITU-T published a Technology Watch Report on the Tactile Internet, which emphasized that scaling up research in the area of wired and wireless access networks would be essential, ushering in new ideas and concepts to boost access networks' redundancy and diversity to meet the stringent latency as well as carrier-grade reliability requirements of Tactile Internet applications [22]. The Tactile Internet provides a medium for remote physical interaction in real-time, which requires the exchange of closed-loop information between virtual or real objects (i.e., humans, machines, and processes). This mandatory end-to-end design approach is fully reflected in the key principles of the reference architecture within the emerging IEEE P1918.1 standards working group (formed in March 2016), which aims to define a framework for the Tactile Internet [23]. Among others, the key principles envision to (i) develop a generic Tactile Internet reference architecture, (ii) support local area as well as wide area connectivity through wireless (e.g., cellular, WiFi) or hybrid wireless and wired networking, and (iii) leverage computing resources from cloud variants at the edge of the network. The working group defines the Tactile Internet as a "network or network of networks for remotely accessing, perceiving, manipulating or controlling real or virtual objects or processes in perceived real-time by humans or machines." Some of the key use cases considered in IEEE P1918.1 include teleoperation, haptic communications, immersive virtual reality, and automotive control.

To give it a more 5G-centric flavor, the Tactile Internet has been more recently also referred to as the 5G-enabled Tactile Internet [24, 25]. Recall that, unlike the previous four cellular generations, future 5G networks will lead to an increasing integration of cellular and WiFi technologies and standards [26]. Furthermore, the importance of the so-called backhaul bottleneck needs to be recognized as well, calling for an end-to-end design approach leveraging both wireless front-end and wired backhaul technologies. Or, as eloquently put by Andrews, the lead author of [26], "placing base stations all over the place is great for providing the mobile stations high-speed access, but does this not just pass the buck to the base stations, which must now somehow get this data to and from the wired core network?" [27]. Clearly, the Tactile Internet opens up a plethora of exciting research directions toward adding a new dimension to the human-to-machine interaction via the Internet. According to the aforementioned ITU-T Technology Watch Report, the Tactile Internet is supposed to be the next leap in the evolution of today's IoT, although there is a significant overlap between 5G, IoT, and the Tactile Internet. For illustration, Fig. 2.3 provides a view of the aforementioned commonalities and differences through the three lenses of IoT, 5G, and the Tactile Internet. The major differences may be best expressed in terms of underlying

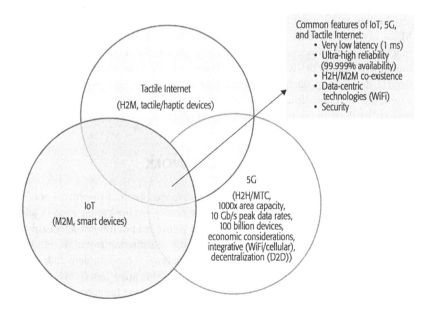

FIGURE 2.3   The three lenses of the Internet of Things (IoT), 5G, and the Tactile Internet: Commonalities and differences.

communications paradigms and enabling devices. IoT relies on M2M communications with a focus on smart devices (e.g., sensors and actuators). In coexistence with emerging MTC, 5G will maintain its traditional human-to-human (H2H) communications paradigm for conventional triple-play services (voice, video, and data) with a growing focus on the integration with other wireless technologies (most notably WiFi) and decentralization. Conversely, the Tactile Internet will be centered on human-to-machine (H2M) communications leveraging tactile and haptic devices. More importantly, despite their differences, IoT, 5G, and the Tactile Internet seem to converge toward a common set of important design goals:

- Very low latency on the order of 1 ms
- Ultra-high reliability with an almost guaranteed availability of 99.999%
- H2H and M2M coexistence
- Integration of data-centric technologies with a particular focus on WiFi
- Security

Importantly, the Tactile Internet involves the inherent human-in-the-loop (HITL) nature of H2M interaction, as opposed to the emerging IoT without any human involvement in its underlying M2M communications. Although M2M communications is useful for the automation of industrial and other machine-centric processes, the Tactile Internet will be centered on human-to-machine/robot (H2M/R) communications and will thus allow for a human-centric design approach toward creating novel immersive experiences and extending the capabilities of the human through the Internet (i.e., augmentation rather than automation of the human) [28].

Human-Agent-Robot Teamwork

A promising approach toward achieving advanced human-machine coordination by means of a superior process for fluidly orchestrating human and machine coactivity may be found in the still young field of human-agent-robot teamwork (HART) research [29]. Unlike early automation research, HART goes beyond the singular focus on full autonomy (i.e., complete independence and self-sufficiency) and cooperative/collaborative autonomy among autonomous systems themselves, which aim at excluding humans as potential teammates for the design of human-out-of-the- loop solutions. In HART, the dynamic allocation of functions and tasks between humans and machines, which may vary over time or be unpredictable in different situations, plays a central role. In particular, with the rise of increasingly smarter machines, the historical humans-are-better-at/machines-are-better-at (HABA/MABA) approach to decide which tasks are best performed by people and which by machines rather than working in concert has become obsolete. To provide a better understanding of the potential and limitations of current smart machines, T. H. Davenport and J. Kirby classified the capabilities of intelligent machines along two dimensions, namely their ability to act and their ability to learn, in their book, *Only Humans Need Apply: Winners and Losers in the Age of Smart Machines*. The ability to act involves four task levels, ranging from the most basic tasks (e.g., analyzing numbers) to performing digital tasks (done by agents) or even physical tasks (done by robots). On the other hand, the ability to learn escalates through four levels, spanning from human-support machines with no inherent intelligence to machines with context awareness, learning, or even self-aware intelligence.

According to Bradshaw et al. [29], among other HART research challenges, the development of capabilities that enable autonomous systems not merely to do things for people but also to work together with people and other systems represents an important open issue to treat humans as "members" of a team of intelligent actors rather than keep viewing them as a conventional "users." In the following, we introduce and extend the concept of fiber-wireless (FiWi) enhanced LTE-advanced (LTE-A) heterogeneous networks (HetNets) to enable both local and non-local teleoperation by exploiting AI-enhanced MEC capabilities to achieve both low round-trip latency and low jitter.

Low-Latency FiWi-Enhanced LTE-A HetNets with AI-Enhanced MEC

Low-latency FiWi-enhanced LTE-A HetNets

FiWi access networks, also referred to as "wireless-optical broadband access networks" (WOBANs), combine the reliability, robustness, and high capacity of optical fiber networks and the flexibility, ubiquity, and cost savings of wireless networks [30]. To deliver peak data rates up to 200 Mbps per user and realize the vision of complete fixed-mobile convergence, it is crucial to replace today's legacy wireline and microwave backhaul technologies with integrated FiWi broadband access networks.

Beyranvand et al. [31] investigated the performance gains obtained from unifying coverage-centric 4G mobile networks and capacity-centric FiWi broadband access networks based on data-centric Ethernet technologies with resulting fiber backhaul sharing and WiFi offloading capabilities in response to the unprecedented growth of mobile data traffic. We evaluated the maximum aggregate throughput, offloading efficiency, and in particular, the delay performance of FiWi-enhanced LTE-A HetNets, including the beneficial impact of various localized fiber-lean backhaul redundancy and wireless protection techniques, by means of probabilistic analysis and verifying simulation. In our study, we paid close attention to fiber backhaul reliability issues stemming from fiber faults of an Ethernet passive optical network (EPON) and WiFi offloading limitations resulting from WiFi mesh node failures as well as temporal and spatial WiFi coverage constraints.

For illustration, Fig. 2.4 depicts the average end-to-end delay performance of FiWi-enhanced LTE-A HetNets versus aggregate throughput for different WiFi offloading ratio (WOR) values, whereby $0 \leq \text{WOR} \leq 1$ denotes the percentage of mobile user traffic offloaded onto WiFi. The presented analytical and verifying simulation results were obtained by assuming a realistic LTE-A and FiWi network configuration under uniform traffic loads and applying minimum (optical and wireless) hop routing. For further details,

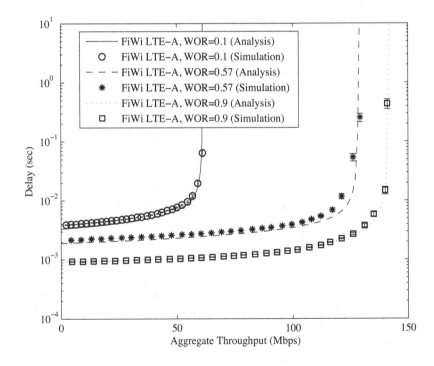

FIGURE 2.4 Average end-to-end delay versus aggregate throughput for different WiFi offloading ratio (WOR).

the interested reader is referred to [31]. For now, let us assume that the reliability of the EPON is ideal (i.e., no fiber backhaul faults occur). However, unlike EPON, the WiFi mesh network may suffer from wireless service outages with a probability of 10−6. We observe from Fig. 2.4 that for increasing WOR the throughput-delay performance of FiWi-enhanced LTE-A HetNets is improved significantly. More precisely, by changing WOR from 0.1 to 0.57 the maximum achievable aggregate throughput increases from about 61 Mbps to roughly 126 Mbps (i.e., the maximum achievable aggregate throughput has more than doubled). More importantly, further increasing WOR to 0.9 does not result in an additional significant increase of the maximum achievable aggregate throughput, but it is instrumental in decreasing the average end-to-end delay and keeping it at a very low level of 10−3 seconds (1 ms) for a wide range of traffic loads. Thus, this result shows that WiFi offloading the majority of data traffic from 4G mobile networks is a promising approach to obtain a very low latency on the order of 1 ms.

AI-enhanced MEC: Pushing AI to the edge

Figure 2.5 depicts the generic network architecture of FiWi-enhanced LTE-A HetNets with an AI-enhanced MEC server. The fiber backhaul consists of

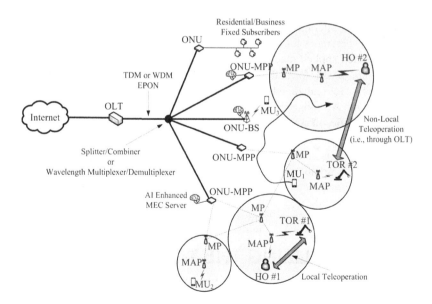

FIGURE 2.5 Architecture of FiWi-based Tactile Internet with artificial intelligence (AI)-enhanced MEC for local and non-local teleoperation.

a time or wavelength division multiplexing (TDM/WDM) IEEE 802.3ah/av 1/10 Gb/s EPON with a typical fiber range of 20 km between the central optical line terminal (OLT) and remote optical network units (ONUs). The EPON may comprise multiple stages, each stage separated by a wavelength-broadcasting splitter and combiner or a wavelength multiplexer and demultiplexer. There are three different subsets of ONUs. An ONU may either serve fixed (wired) subscribers. Alternatively, it may connect to a cellular network base station (BS) or an IEEE 802.11n/ac/s WLAN mesh portal point (MPP), giving rise to a collocated ONU-BS or ONU-MPP, respectively. Depending on the trajectory, a mobile user (MU) may communicate through the cellular network or WLAN mesh front end, which consists of ONU-MPPs, intermediate mesh points (MPs), and mesh access points (MAPs) [32].

Human operators (HOs) and teleoperator robots (TORs) are assumed to communicate only via WLAN, as opposed to MUs using their dual-mode 4G/WiFi smartphones. Teleoperation is done either locally or non-locally, depending on the proximity of the involved HO and TOR, as illustrated in Fig. 2.5. In local teleoperation, the HO and corresponding TOR are associated with the same MAP and exchange their command and feedback samples through this MAP without traversing the fiber backhaul. Conversely, if HO and TOR are associated with different MAPs, non-local teleoperation is generally done by communicating via the backhaul EPON and central OLT. Despite recent interest in exploiting machine learning for optical communications and networking, edge intelligence for enabling an immersive and transparent teleoperation experiences for HOs has not been explored yet. In [32], Maier and Ebrahimzadeh applied machine learning at the edge of our considered communication network for realizing immersive and frictionless Tactile Internet experiences. To realize edge intelligence, selected ONU- BSs/MPPs are equipped with AI-enhanced MEC servers. These servers rely on the computational capabilities of cloudlets collocated at the optical-wireless interface (see Fig. 2.5) to forecast delayed haptic samples in the feedback path. As a consequence, the HO is enabled to perceive the remote task environment in real-time at a 1-ms granularity, thus resulting in tighter togetherness, improved safety control, and increased reliability of the teleoperation systems.

DECENTRALIZING THE TACTILE INTERNET

Recall from the "Introduction" that the Tactile Internet will involve the inherent HITL nature of H2M interaction, as opposed to the emerging IoT. Thus, it allows for a human-centric design approach toward extending the capabilities of the human through the Internet for the augmentation rather than automation of the human. Recently, Maier et al. [28] put forward the idea that the Tactile Internet may be the harbinger of human augmentation and human-machine symbiosis envisioned by contemporary and early-day Internet pioneers. More specifically, we elaborated the role AI-enhanced agents may play in supporting humans in their task coordination between humans and machines. Toward achieving advanced human-machine coordination, we developed a distributed allocation algorithm of computational and physical tasks for fluidly orchestrating HART coactivities (e.g., the shared use of user- and/or network-owned robots). In our design approach, all HART members established through communication a collective self-awareness with the objective of minimizing the task completion time.

In the following, we search for synergies between the aforementioned HART membership and the complementary strengths of the DAO, AI, and robots (see Fig. 2.2) to facilitate local human-machine coactivity clusters by decentralizing the Tactile Internet. Toward this end, it is important to better understand the merits and limits of AI. Recently, Stanford University launched its *One Hundred Year Study on Artificial Intelligence (AI100)*. In the inaugural report "Artificial Intelligence and Life in 2030," the authors defined AI as a set of computational technologies that are inspired by the ways people use their nervous systems and bodies to sense, learn, reason, and take action. They also point out that AI will likely replace tasks rather than jobs in the near term and highlight the importance of crowdsourcing human expertise to solve problems that computers alone cannot solve well.

Decentralized Edge Intelligence

First, let us explore the potential of leveraging mobile end-user equipment by partially or fully decentralizing MEC. We introduce the use of AI-enhanced MEC servers at the optical-wireless interface of converged fiber-wireless mobile networks for computation offloading. Assuming the same default network parameter setting and simulation setup as in [28], we consider $1 \leq N_{Edge} \leq 4$ AI-enhanced MEC servers, each associated with 8 end users, whereof $1 \leq N_{PD} \leq 8$ partially decentralized end users can flexibly control the number of offloaded tasks by varying their computation offloading probability. The remaining $8 - N_{PD}$ are fully centralized end users that rely on edge computing only (i.e., their computation offloading probability equals 1). Note that for $N_{Edge} = 4$, all end users may offload their computation tasks onto an edge node. Conversely, for $N_{Edge} < 4$, one or more edge nodes are unavailable for computation offloading and their associated end users fall back on their local computation resources (i.e., fully decentralized). Figure 2.6 shows the average task completion time versus computation offloading probability of the partially decentralized end users

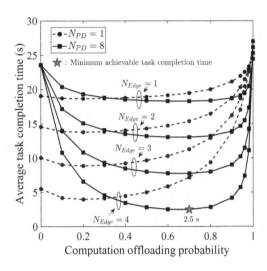

FIGURE 2.6 Average task completion time (in seconds) versus computation offloading probability for different numbers of partially decentralized end users (n_{PD}) and artificial intelligence (AI)-enhanced MEC servers (n_{edge}).

for different N_{Edge} and N_{PD}. We observe from Fig. 2.6 that for a given N_{Edge}, increasing N_{PD} (i.e., higher level of decentralization) is effective in reducing the average task completion time. Specifically, for $N_{Edge} = 4$, a high decentralization level ($N_{PD} = 8$) allows end users to experience a reduction of the average task completion time of up to 89.5% by optimally adjusting their computation offloading probability to 0.7.

As interconnected computing power has spread around the world and useful platforms have been built on top of it, the crowd has become a demonstrably viable and valuable resource. According to McAfee and Brynjolfsson [6], there are many ways for companies that are squarely at the core of modern capitalism to tap into the expertise of uncredentialed and conventionally inexperienced members of the technology-enabled crowd such as the DAO. Maier et al. [28] developed a self-aware allocation algorithm of physical tasks for HART-centric task coordination based on the shared use of user- and network-owned robots. Recall from "AI-Enhanced MEC: Pushing AI to the Edge" that by using our AI-enhanced MEC servers as autonomous agents, we showed that delayed force feedback samples coming from TORs may be locally generated and delivered to HOs in close proximity. Note, however, that the performance of the sample forecasting-based teleoperation system heavily relies on the accuracy of the forecast algorithm.

Crowdsourcing: Expanding the HO Workforce

Toward realizing DAO in a decentralized Tactile Internet, Ethereum may be used to establish HO-TOR sessions for remote physical task execution, whereby smart contracts help establish and maintain trusted HART membership and allow each HART member to have global knowledge about all participating HOs, TORs, and MEC servers that act as autonomous agents following the widely used gateway-oriented approach (see Blockchain IoT (B-IoT): Recent Progress and Related Work). An HO remotely executes a given physical task until k out of the recent n haptic feedback samples are misforecast. At this point, the HO immediately stops the teleoperation and informs the agent. The agent assigns the interrupted task to an available HO in the vicinity, who then traverses to the task point and finalizes the physical task. For $n = 5$, Fig. 2.7 depicts the average task completion time versus the probability of sample misforecast for different k and f_{human}/f_{robot}, where f_{human} and f_{robot} denote the capability (in terms of number of operations per second) of a human and robot for performing physical tasks, respectively. We observe that the task completion time increases as the probability of sample misforecast grows from 0 to 0.25 for $k = 1$, whereas it remains almost unchanged for $k = 3$. Further, note that as humans become more capable (i.e., increasing f_{human}/f_{robot}), the resultant task completion time decreases until it hits a plateau, as traversing incurs additional delays.

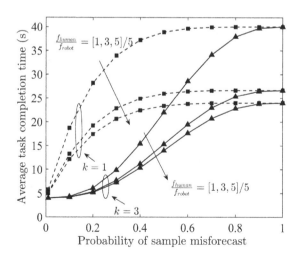

FIGURE 2.7 Average task completion time (in seconds) versus the probability of sample misforecast for different number of misforecasts (k) and ratio of human and robot operational capabilities (f_{human}/f_{robot}).

BLOCKCHAIN, AI, AND HUMAN INTELLIGENCE: THE PATH FORWARD

Today, AI, machine learning, robots, and IoT are converging to create a new wave of change as they begin to take advantage of cryptocurrencies, initial coin offerings (ICOs), virtual assets, and tokenization of everything.

The outcome of this convergence of innovations and human cause fears about job loss, robot overlords, and the future in general [33].

Maier et al. [28] touched on the importance of shifting the research focus from AI to intelligence amplification (IA) by using information technology to enhance human decisions. Note, however, that IA becomes difficult in dynamic task environments of increased uncertainty and real-world situations of great complexity. IA, also known as "cognitive augmentation" or "machine-augmented intelligence," will be instrumental in enhancing the creativity, understanding, efficiency, and intelligence of humans.

Cognitive-Assistance-Based Intelligence Amplification

Edge computing is a widely studied approach to increase the usefulness of crowdsourcing, which may be used to guide humans step-by-step through the physical task execution process by providing them with cognitive assistance. Technically, this could be easily realized by equipping an unskilled DAO member with an augmented reality (AR) headset (e.g., HoloLens 2 with WiFi connectivity) that receives work-order information in real time from its nearest AI-enhanced MEC server.

HITL Hybrid-Augmented Intelligence

Many problems that humans face tend to be of high uncertainty, complexity, and open-ended. To solve such problems, human interaction and participation may be introduced. As a result, this gives rise to the concept of HITL hybrid-augmented intelligence for advanced human-machine collaboration [34]. HITL hybrid-augmented intelligence is defined as an intelligent model that requires human interaction and allows for addressing problems and requirements that may not be easily trained or classified by machine learning. In general, machine learning is inferior to the human brain in understanding unstructured real-world environments and processing incomplete information and complex spatiotemporal correlation tasks. Hence, machines cannot carry out all the tasks in human society on their own. Instead, AI and human intelligence are better viewed as highly complementary.

According to Zheng et al. [34], the Internet provides an immense innovation space for HITL hybrid-augmented intelligence. Specifically, cloud robotics and AR are among the fastest-growing commercial applications for enhancing the intelligence of an individual in multi-robot collaborative systems. One of the main research topics of HITL hybrid-augmented intelligence is the development of methods that allow machines to learn from not only massive training samples but also human knowledge to accomplish highly intelligent tasks via shared intelligence among different robots and humans.

The Rise of the Decentralized Self-Organizing Cooperative

A very interesting example to catalyze human and machine intelligence toward a new form of self-organizing artificial general intelligence (AGI) across the Internet is the so-called SingularityNET.[1] One can think of SingularityNet as a decentralized self-organizing cooperative (DSOC), a concept similar to the aforementioned DAO. DSOC is essentially a distributed computing architecture for making new kinds of smart contracts. Entities executing these smart contracts are referred to as "agents," which can run in the cloud, on phones, robots, or other embedded devices. Services are offered to any customer via APIs enabled by smart contracts and may require a combination of actions by multiple agents using their collective intelligence. In general, there may be multiple agents that can fulfill a given task request in different ways and to different degrees. Each task request to the network requires a unique combination of agents, thus forming a so-called "offer network of mutual dependency," where agents make offers to each other to exchange services via offer-request pairs. Whenever someone wants an agent to perform services, a smart contract is signed for this specific task. Toward this end, DSOC aims at leveraging contributions from the broadest possible variety of agents by means of superior discovery mechanisms for finding useful agents and nudging them to become contributors.

Nudging toward Human Augmentation

Extending on the DSOC concept, we advocate the use of the nudge theory for enhancing the human capabilities of unskilled crowd members of the DAO. According to Richard H. Thaler, the 2017 Nobel Laureate in Economics, the nudge theory claims that positive reinforcement and indirect suggestions can influence the behavior of groups and individuals. A suitable nudging mechanism aims at completing interrupted local physical tasks by learning from a remote skilled DAO member, who is able to transfer her knowledge as data via a secure blockchain transaction embedded in a smart contract with an appropriate reward for each sub-task. This smart contract will initially enhance the local HO's capability, thereby allowing it to successfully accomplish a given task via shared intelligence among failing robots and skilled humans.

OPEN CHALLENGES AND FUTURE WORK

The Internet has been constantly evolving from the mobile Internet to the emerging IoT and future Tactile Internet. Similarly, the capabilities of future 5G networks will extend far beyond those of previous generations of mobile communication. By boosting access networks' redundancy and diversity as envisioned in ITU-T [22], FiWi-enhanced 4G LTE-A HetNets with AI-embedded MEC hold great promise to meet the stringent latency and reliability requirements of immersive Tactile Internet applications. Maier [35] recently outlined some research ideas that help tap into the full potential of the Tactile Internet. However, other concepts such as the discussed spreading ownership, DAO, and HART membership will be instrumental in ushering in new ideas and concepts to facilitate local human-machine coactivity clusters by completely decentralizing edge computing via emerging Ethereum blockchain technologies to realize future techno-social systems such as the Tactile Internet, which by design still requires heavy involvement from humans at the network edge instead of automating them away. More work lies ahead to integrate Ethernet-based FiWi-enhanced mobile networks with Ethereum blockchain technologies. Although blockchain technology is promising technology to enhance today's IoT, there are still many research issues to be addressed before the integration of blockchain with IoT, especially in future mobile networks (i.e., 6G and beyond) that play a primordial role in constructing the underlying infrastructure for blockchains.

CONCLUSIONS

In this chapter, we showed that many of the emerging B-IoT studies use Ethereum as the blockchain of choice and apply a gateway-oriented design approach to offload computationally intensive tasks from resource-constrained end devices onto an intermediate gateway, thus enabling them to access the Ethereum blockchain network. Building on our recent Tactile Internet work on orchestrating hybrid HART coactivities, we showed that higher levels of decentralized AI-enhanced MEC are effective in reducing the average completion time of computational tasks. Further, for remote execution of physical tasks in a decentralized Tactile Internet, we explored how Ethereum's DAO and smart contracts may be used to establish trusted HART membership and how human crowdsourcing helps decrease physical task completion time in the event of unreliable forecasting of haptic feedback samples from teleoperated robots. We outlined future research avenues on technological convergence to successfully accomplish hybrid machine-human tasks by tapping into the shared intelligence of the crowd.

NOTE

1. SingularityNET Whitepaper, "SingularityNET: A decentralized, open market and internetwork for AIs," November 2017. https://singularitynet.io.

REFERENCES

1. M. Maier, M. Chowdhury, B. P. Rimal and D. P. Van, "The Tactile Internet: Vision, Recent Progress, and Open Challenges," *IEEE Communications Magazine*, vol. 54, no. 5, pp. 138–145, 2016.
2. D. Tapscott and A. Tapscott, *Blockchain Revolution: How the Technology Behind Bitcoin Is Changing Money, Business, and the World*, Portfolio, Penguin, Toronto, 2016.
3. W. Saad, M. Bennis and M. Chen, "A Vision of 6G Wireless Systems: Applications, Trends, Technologies, and Open Research Problems," Preprint, *arXiv:1902.10265*, 2019.
4. T. Salman, M. Zolanvari, A. Erbad, R. Jain and M. Samaka, "Security Services Using Blockchains: A State of the Art Survey," *IEEE Communications Surveys & Tutorials*, vol. 21, no. 1, pp. 858–880, 2019.
5. V. Buterin, "A Next-Generation Smart Contract and Decentralized Application Platform," *Ethereum White Paper*, www.ethereum.org.
6. A. McAfee and E. Brynjolfsson, *Machine, Platform, Crowd: Harnessing Our Digital Future*, W. W. Norton, New York, NY, 2017.
7. F. Tschorsch and B. Scheuermann, "Bitcoin and Beyond: A Technical Survey on Decentralized Digital Currencies," *IEEE Communications Surveys & Tutorials*, vol. 18, no. 3, pp. 2084–2123, 2016.

8. R. Beck, "Beyond Bitcoin: The Rise of Blockchain World," *IEEE Computer*, vol. 51, no. 2, pp. 54–58, 2018.

9. O. Novo, "Blockchain Meets IoT: An Architecture for Scalable Access Management in IoT," *IEEE Internet of Things Journal*, vol. 5, no. 2, pp. 1184–1195, 2018.

10. Y. N. Aung and T. Tantidham, "Review of Ethereum: Smart Home Case Study," *Proceedings of the 2nd International Conference on Information Technology (INCIT)*, Nakhon Pathom, Thailand, 2017, pp. 1–4.

11. C. F. Liao, S. W. Bao, C. J. Cheng and K. Chen, "On Design Issues and Architectural Styles for Blockchain-Driven IoT Services," *Proceedings of the IEEE International Conference on Consumer Electronics-Taiwan (ICCE-TW)*, Taipei, 2017, pp. 351–352.

12. P. Urien, "Toward Secure Elements for Trusted Transactions in Blockchain and Blockchain IoT (BIoT) Platforms," *Proceedings of the Fourth International Conference on Mobile and Secure Services (MobiSecServ)*, Miami Beach, FL, 2018, pp. 1–5.

13. G. C. Polyzos and N. Fotiou, "Blockchain-Assisted Information Distribution for the Internet of Things," *Proceedings of the IEEE International Conference on Information Reuse and Integration (IRI)*, San Diego, CA, 2017, pp. 75–78.

14. Y. Gupta, R. Shorey, D. Kulkarni and J. Tew, "The Applicability of Blockchain in the Internet of Things," *Proceedings of the 10th International Conference on Communication Systems & Networks (COMSNETS)*, Bengaluru, India, 2018, pp. 561–564.

15. K. R. Özyilmaz and A. Yurdakul, "Work-in-Progress: Integrating Low-Power IoT Devices to a Blockchain-Based Infrastructure," *Proceedings of the International Conference on Embedded Software (EMSOFT)*, Seoul, South Korea, 2017, pp. 1–2.

16. X. Duan, Z. Yan, G. Geng and B. Yan, "DNSLedger: Decentralized and Distributed Name Resolution for Ubiquitous IoT," *Proceedings of the IEEE International Conference on Consumer Electronics (ICCE)*, Las Vegas, NV, 2018, pp. 1–3.

17. R. Yang, F. R. Yu, P. Si, Z. Yang and Y. Zhang, "Integrated Blockchain and Edge Computing Systems: A Survey, Some Research Issues and Challenges," *IEEE Communications Surveys & Tutorials*, vol. 21, no. 2, pp. 1508–1532, 2019.

18. J. Pan, J. Wang, A. Hester, I. Alqerm, Y. Liu and Y. Zhao, "EdgeChain: An Edge- IoT Framework and Prototype Based on Blockchain and Smart Contracts," *IEEE Internet of Things Journal*, vol. 6, no. 3, pp. 4719–4732, 2019.

19. X. Xu, X. Zhang, H. Gao, Y. Xue, L. Qi and W. Dou, "BeCome: Blockchain-Enabled Computation Offloading for IoT in Mobile Edge Computing," *IEEE Transactions on Industrial Informatics*, vol. 16, no. 6, pp. 4187–4195, 2020, doi:10.1109/TII.2019.2936869.

20. M. Zhaofeng, W. Xiaochang, D. K. Jain, H. Khan, G. Hongmin and W. Zhen, "A Blockchain-Based Trusted Data Management Scheme in Edge Computing," *IEEE Transactions on Industrial Informatics*, vol. 16, no. 3, pp. 2013–2021, 2020, doi:10.1109/TII.2019.2933482.

21. G. P. Fettweis, "The Tactile Internet: Applications and Challenges," *IEEE Vehicular Technology Magazine*, vol. 9, no. 1, pp. 64–70, 2014.

22. ITU-T, "The Tactile Internet," International Telecommunication Union (ITU), Technology Watch Report, August 2014. [Online]. Available: https://www.itu.int/dms pub/itu-t/oth/23/01/T23010000230001PDFE.pdf.

23. A. Aijaz, Z. Dawy, N. Pappas, M. Simsek, S. Oteafy and O. Holland, "Toward a Tactile Internet Reference Architecture: Vision and Progress of the IEEE P1918.1 Standard," Preprint, *arXiv:1807.11915*, 2018.

24. M. Simsek, A. Aijaz, M. Dohler, J. Sachs and G. Fettweis, "5G-enabled Tactile Internet," *IEEE Journal of Selected Areas in Communications*, vol. 34, no. 3, pp. 460–473, 2016.

25. A. Aijaz, M. Dohler, A. H. Aghvami, V. Friderikos and M. Frodigh, "Realizing the Tactile Internet: Haptic Communications Over Next Generation 5G Cellular Networks," *IEEE Wireless Communications*, vol. 24, no. 2, pp. 82–89, 2017.

26. J. G. Andrews, S. Buzzi, W. Choi, S. V. Hanley, A. Lozano, A. C. K. Soong and J. C. Zhang, "What Will 5G Be?" *IEEE Journal of Selected Areas in Communications*, vol. 32, no. 6, pp. 1065–1082, 2014.

27. J. G. Andrews, "Seven Ways that HetNets Are a Cellular Paradigm Shift," *IEEE Communications Magazine*, vol. 51, no. 3, pp. 136–144, 2013.

28. M. Maier, A. Ebrahimzadeh and M. Chowdhury, "The Tactile Internet: Automation or Augmentation of the Human?" *IEEE Access*, vol. 6, pp. 41607–41618, 2018.

29. J. M. Bradshaw, V. Dignum, C. Jonker and M. Sierhuis, "Human-Agent-Robot Teamwork," *IEEE Intelligent Systems*, vol. 27, no. 2, pp. 8–13, 2012.

30. F. Aurzada, M. Lévesque, M. Maier and M. Reisslein, "FiWi Access Networks Based on Next-Generation PON and Gigabit-Class WLAN Technologies: A Capacity and Delay Analysis," *IEEE/ACM Transactions on Networking*, vol. 22, no. 4, pp. 1176–1189, 2014.

31. H. Beyranvand, M. Lévesque, M. Maier and J. A. Salehi, "FiWi Enhanced LTE-A HetNets with Unreliable Fiber Backhaul Sharing and WiFi Offloading," *Proceedings of the IEEE INFOCOM*, Hong Kong, 2015, pp. 1275–1283.

32. M. Maier and A. Ebrahimzadeh, "Toward Immersive Tactile Internet Experiences: Low-Latency FiWi Enhanced Mobile Networks with Edge Intelligence [Invited]," *IEEE/OSA Journal of Optical Communications and Networking, Special Issue on Latency in Edge Optical Networks*, vol. 11, no. 4, pp. B10–B25, 2019.

33. A. Pentland, J. Werner and C. Bishop, "Blockchain+AI+Human: Whitepaper and Invitation," MIT Press, 2018. [Online]. Available: https://connection.mit.edu/sites/default/files/publication-pdfs/blockchain%2BAI%2BHumans.pdf.

34. N. Zheng, Z. Liu, P. Ren, Y. Ma, S. Chen, S. Yu, J. Xue, B. Chen and F. Wang, "Hybrid-Augmented Intelligence: Collaboration and Cognition," *Frontiers of Information Technology & Electronic Engineering*, vol. 18, no. 2, pp. 153–179, 2017.

35. M. Maier, "The Tactile Internet: Where Do We Go from Here? (Invited Paper)," *IEEE/OSA/SPIE Asia Communications and Photonics (ACP) Conference*, Hangzhou, China, 2018.

DAO-Based Trusted Collaboration and Social Cohesion Approach for the 6G-Tactile Internet

3

INTRODUCTION

We have seen in Chapter 2 that there has been a growing interest in adapting blockchain to the specific needs of the Internet of Things (IoT) in order to develop a variety of blockchain Iot (B-IoT) applications, ranging from smart cities and Industry 4.0 to financial transactions and farming, among others. Toward this end, the authors of [1] pointed out the important role of smart contracts, which are defined as pieces of self-sufficient decentralized code that are executed autonomously when certain conditions are met, whereby Ethereum was one of the first blockchains using smart contracts. The use of Ethereum allows users to write and run their own code on top of the network. By updating the code, users are able to modify the behavior of IoT devices

DOI: 10.1201/9781003427322-3

for simplified maintenance and error correction. Besides well-known B-IoT problems such as hosting a blockchain on resource-constrained IoT devices, low transaction rates, and long block creation times, Fernández-Caramés and Fraga-Lamas [1] identified several significant challenges beyond early B-IoT developments and deployments that will need further investigation. Apart from technological challenges, e.g., access control and security, the authors concluded that shaping the regulatory environment, e.g., *decentralized ownership*, is one of the biggest issues to unlock the potential of B-IoT for its broader use.

Recently, in [2], gateways were used to act as B-IoT service agents for their respective cluster of local resource-constrained IoT devices by storing their blockchain accounts and using them to execute smart contracts on their behalf. The proposed smart contract-based framework consists of multiple access control contracts (ACCs). Each ACC maintains a misbehavior list for each B-IoT resource, including details and time of the misbehavior as well as the penalty on its subject, e.g., blocking access requests for a certain period of time. Further, in addition to a register contract, the framework involves the so-called *judge contract (JC)*, which implements a certain misbehavior judging method. After receiving the misbehavior reports from the ACCs, the JC determines the penalty on the corresponding subjects and returns the decisions to the ACCs for execution.

Despite the recent progress, the salient features that set Ethereum aside from other blockchains remain to be explored in more depth, including their symbiosis with other emerging key technologies such as AI and robots apart from decentralized edge computing solutions. A question of particular interest hereby is how decentralized blockchain mechanisms may be leveraged to let emerge new hybrid forms of collaboration among individuals, which haven't been entertained in the traditional market-oriented economy dominated by firms rather than individuals [3]. Of particular interest will be Ethereum's concept of decentralized autonomous organizations (DAO). In fact, in their latest book on how to harness our digital future [4], Andrew McAfee and Erik Brynjolfsson speak of "The Way of The DAO" which may substitute a technology-enabled crowd for traditional organizations such as companies.

While fifth generation (5G) networks have not been widely deployed yet, early studies have already started to look beyond 5G networks and speculate what the future sixth generation (6G) vision might be. Unlike 5G, 6G will not only explore more spectrum at high-frequency bands, but converge driving technological trends. Saad et al. [5] argue that there will be the following three driving applications behind 6G: (*i*) blockchain and distributed ledger technologies, (*ii*) connected robots and autonomous systems, and (*iii*) wireless brain-computer interaction (a subclass of human-machine interaction). In this chapter, we focus on the Tactile Internet, which is supposed to be the next leap in the evolution of today's IoT. Note that the IoT with its underlying machine-to-machine (M2M) communications is useful for enabling the automation of industrial and other machine-centric processes. It is designed to enable communications among machines without relying on any human involvement. Conversely, the Tactile Internet will add a new dimension to human-to-machine (H2M) interaction involving its inherent human-in-the-loop (HITL) nature, thus allowing for a human-centric design approach toward creating novel immersive experiences and extending the capabilities of the human through the Internet, i.e., augmentation rather than automation of the human [6]. This chapter aims at addressing the open research challenges outlined above.

Maier and Ebrahimzadeh [6] covered various important aspects of the Tactile Internet (i.e., haptic traffic characterization and edge intelligence), but outlined future work on the blockchain only briefly. In this chapter, we build on our findings in [6] and make the following contributions: (*i*) investigate the potential of leveraging mobile end-user equipment for decentralization via blockchain, (*ii*) explore how crowdsourcing may be used to decrease the completion time of physical tasks, and (*iii*) extend the B-IoT framework from judge contract to nudge contract for enabling the nudging of human users in a broader Tactile Internet context.

The remainder of the chapter is structured as follows. "Decentralizing the Tactile Internet" section elaborates on the potential role of Ethereum and in particular the DAO in helping decentralize the Tactile Internet. In "Nudging: From Judge Contract to Nudge Contract" section, we explore possibilities to extend the B-IoT framework of judge contract to nudge contract for enabling the *nudging* of human users in a broader Tactile Internet context. Finally, "Conclusions" section concludes the chapter.

DECENTRALIZING THE TACTILE INTERNET

FiWi Enhanced Mobile Networks: Spreading Ownership

Maier and Ebrahimzadeh [6] have shown that the 5G ultra-reliable and low latency communications (URLLC) requirements can be achieved by enhancing coverage-centric 4G LTE-A HetNets with capacity-centric FiWi access networks based on low-cost, data-centric EPON and WLAN technologies in the backhaul and front-end, respectively. Figure 3.1 illustrates

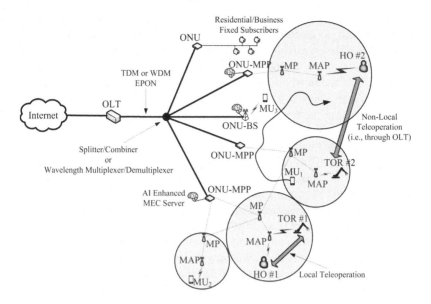

FIGURE 3.1   Architecture of FiWi enhanced mobile networks with AI-enhanced MEC for immersive Tactile Internet applications.

the architecture of such FiWi-enhanced mobile networks in greater detail. The common EPON fiber backhaul is shared by a number of optical network units (ONUs), which may either connect to fixed subscribers or interface with a WLAN MPP or a cellular BS. Some of the resultant ONU-MPPs/ONU-BSs may be equipped with an AI-enhanced MEC server (to be described in more detail shortly). On the end-user side, we consider the following three types of subscribers: conventional MUs as well as pairs of HO and TOR involved in teleoperation, which may be either local or non-local.

More interestingly to this chapter, note that Maier and Ebrahimzadeh [6] explored the idea of treating the human as a "member" of a team of intelligent machines rather than keep viewing him as a conventional "user." In addition, we elaborated on the role AI-enhanced agents (e.g., MEC servers) may play in supporting humans in their task coordination between humans and machines. Toward achieving advanced human-machine coordination, we developed a distributed allocation algorithm of computational and physical tasks for fluidly orchestrating hybrid HART coactivities. More specifically, all HART members established through communication a collective self-awareness with the objective of minimizing the task completion time based on the shared use of robots that may be either user- or network-owned. We were particularly interested in the impact of *spreading ownership* of robots among people whose work they may replace. Our results showed that from a performance perspective (in terms of task completion time) no deterioration occurs if the ownership of robots is shifted entirely from network operators to mobile users, though spreading ownership across end-users makes a huge difference in who reaps the benefits from new technologies such as robots. This also applies to blockchain technologies, of course. Recall from the "Introduction" section that decentralized ownership is one of the biggest issues to unlock the potential of B-IoT for its broader use.

Given that 6G will support new service types, e.g., computation-oriented communications (CoC) [7], where new smart devices call for distributed computation, we search for synergies between the aforementioned HART membership and the complementary strengths of the DAO, AI, and robots to facilitate local human-machine coactivity clusters by decentralizing the Tactile Internet. Toward this end, it's important to better understand the merits and limits of AI. Recently, Stanford University launched its *One Hundred Year Study on Artificial Intelligence (AI100)*. In the inaugural report "Artificial Intelligence and Life in 2030," the authors defined AI as a set of computational technologies that are inspired by the ways people use their nervous systems and bodies to sense, learn, reason, and take action. They also point out that AI will likely replace tasks rather than jobs in the near term and highlight the importance of *crowdsourcing* of human expertise to solve problems that computers alone cannot solve well. As interconnected computing power has spread around the world and useful platforms have been built on top of it, the crowd has become a demonstrably viable and valuable resource. According to McAfee and Brynjolfsson [4], there are many ways for companies that are squarely at the core of modern capitalism to tap into the expertise of uncredentialed and conventionally inexperienced members of the technology-enabled crowd such as the DAO.

AI-Enhanced MEC

According to [7], 6G will go beyond mobile Internet and will be required to support ubiquitous AI services from the core to the end devices. In the following, we explore the potential of leveraging mobile end-user equipment by partially or fully decentralizing MEC. Recall from above that we introduced the use of AI-enhanced MEC servers at the optical-wireless interface of FiWi-enhanced mobile networks. In our considered scenario, we assume that the human-system interface (HSI) at the human operator side is equipped with the so-called AI-enabled edge sample forecasting module (ESF), which is responsible to provide the human operator with the predicted samples if the samples are lost or excessively delayed. This as a result helps the human operator have a transparent perception of the remote environment. In a B-IoT context, these MEC servers have been used as gateways that are required to act as B-IoT service agents to release resource-constrained IoT devices from computation-intensive tasks by offloading blockchain transactions onto more powerful edge computing resources, as discussed in the "Introduction" section. This design constraint can be relaxed in the Tactile Internet, where the user equipment (e.g., state-of-the-art smartphones or the aforementioned user-owned robots) is computationally more resourceful than IoT devices and thus may be exploited for decentralization.

In our simulations, we set the FiWi network parameters as follows: Distributed Coordination Function Interframe Space (DIFS) = 34 μsec, Short Interframe Space (SIFS) = 16 μsec, Physical Layer (PHY) Header = 20 μsec, W0 = 16 μsec, H = 6, E = 9 μsec, Request To Send (RTS) = 20 bytes, Clear To Send (CTS) = 14 bytes, Acknowledgment (ACK) = 14 bytes, rWMN = 300 Mbps, cPON = 10 Gbps, PON fiber reach lPON = 20 Km, average packet length L = 1500 bytes, $\varsigma_L^2 = 0$, ONU-AP radius = 102 m. We also consider $1 \leq$ NEdge ≤ 4 AI-enhanced MEC servers, each associated with 8 end-users, whereof $1 \leq$ NP D ≤ 8 partially decentralized end-users can flexibly control the number of offloaded tasks by varying their computation offloading probability. The remaining 8—NP D are fully centralized end-users that rely on edge computing only (i.e., their computation offloading probability equals 1). Note that for NEdge = 4, all end-users may offload their computation tasks onto an edge node. Conversely, for NEdge < 4, one or more edge nodes are unavailable for computation offloading and their associated end-users fall back on their local computation resources (i.e., fully decentralized). The computational capacity of MEC servers and partially decentralized end-users are set to 1.44 GHz and 185 MHz, respectively. For a more detailed description of the system model, parameter setting, and network configuration, the interested reader is referred to Maier and Ebrahimzadeh [6]. Figure 3.2 shows the average task completion time vs. computation offloading probability of the partially decentralized end-users for different NEdge and NP D. We observe from Fig. 3.2 that for a given NEdge, increasing NP D (i.e., higher level of decentralization) is effective in reducing the average task completion time. Specifically, for NEdge = 4, a high decentralization level (NP D = 8) allows end-users to experience a reduction of the average task completion time of up to 89.5% by optimally adjusting their computation offloading probability to 0.7. As shown in Fig. 3.2, increasing NP D results in not only a decrease of the average execution time but also a decrease of the communication overhead/burden in the wireless fronthaul of our considered FiWi network, as a larger number of users shift the computation load from the MEC servers toward their local CPUs.

Note that in Fig. 3.2, the average task completion time is on the order of seconds, ranging from 2.5 to 25 seconds depending on the computation offloading

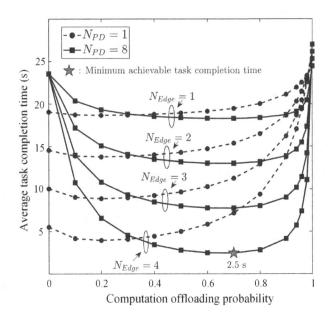

FIGURE 3.2 Average computational task completion time (in seconds) vs. computation offloading probability for different numbers of partially decentralized end-users (*NPD*) and AI-enhanced MEC servers (n_{edge}).

probability. Hence, given Ethereum's transaction limit of 20 transactions/second, the notoriously low transaction rate of blockchain technologies doesn't pose a significant challenge to the execution of computational tasks and especially physical tasks carried out by robots in the context of the Tactile Internet, given that the mining process anticipated to be performed by a local CPU of a robot will be offloaded to a nearby MEC server to increase both task completion and transaction confirmation times.

CROWDSOURCING

Maier and Ebrahimzadeh [6] developed a self-aware allocation algorithm of physical tasks for HART-centric task coordination based on the shared use of user- and network-owned robots. By using our AI-enhanced MEC servers as autonomous agents, we showed that delayed force feedback samples coming from TORs may be locally generated and delivered to HOs in close proximity.

More specifically, we developed an artificial neural network (ANN) based forecasting scheme of delayed (or lost) force feedback samples. By delivering the forecast samples to the HO rather than waiting for the delayed ones, we showed that AI-enhanced MEC servers enable HOs to perceive the remote physical task environment in real-time at a 1-millisecond granularity and thus achieve tighter togetherness and improved safety control therein. Note, however, that the performance of the sample forecasting-based teleoperation system heavily relies on the accuracy of the forecast algorithm.

In the following, we explore how crowdsourcing helps decrease the completion time of physical tasks in the event of unreliable forecasting of force feedback samples from TORs. Toward realizing DAO in a decentralized Tactile Internet, Ethereum may be used to establish HO-TOR sessions for remote physical task execution, whereby smart contracts help establish/maintain trusted HART membership and allow each HART member to have global knowledge about all participating HOs, TORs, and MEC servers that act as autonomous agents. We assume that an HO remotely executes a given physical task until X% of the most recently received haptic feedback samples are misforecast. At this point, the HO immediately stops the teleoperation and informs the agent. The agent assigns the interrupted task to a nearby human (e.g., an available HO) in the vicinity of the TOR, who then traverses to the task point and finalizes the physical task. The probability of misforecast for a given ESF implementation can be quantified by calculating the long-run average of the ratio of the number of samples that are subject to misforecast to the number of those that are predicted correctly. Figure 3.3 depicts the average task completion time vs. probability of sample misforecast for different traverse time $T_{traverse}$ of the nearby human and different ratio of human and robot operational capabilities $\frac{f_{human}}{f_{robot}}$, where f_{human} and f_{robot} denote the number of operations per second a human and robot is capable of performing, respectively. We can make several observations from Fig. 3.3. Obviously, it is beneficial to select humans with a shorter traverse time, who happen to be closer to the interrupted TOR. We also observe that the ratio $\frac{f_{human}}{f_{robot}}$ has a significant impact on the average task completion time. Clearly, for a ratio of smaller than 1 (i.e., 1/3), human assistance is less useful since it takes him/her more time to complete the physical task. Conversely, for a ratio equal to 1 (i.e., 3/3) and especially larger than 1 (i.e., 5/3), crowdsourcing pays off by making use of the superior operational capabilities of the human. Whether humans or robots are better suited to perform a physical task certainly depends on its nature. However, for a given physical task, an interesting approach to benefit from the assistance of even uncredentialed and inexperienced crowd members of the DAO may be to enhance the capabilities of humans by means of *nudging*, as explained next.

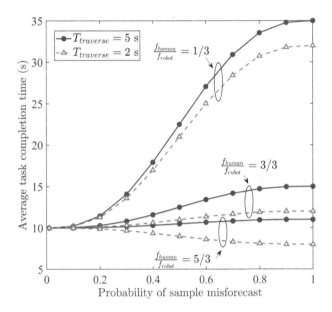

FIGURE 3.3   Average physical task completion time (in seconds) vs. probability of sample misforecast for different traverse time t$_{traverse}$ ∈ {2, 5} seconds of nearby human and different ratio of human and robot operational capabilities $\frac{f_{human}}{f_{robot}}$ (for X = 80% fixed).

NUDGING: FROM JUDGE CONTRACT TO NUDGE CONTRACT

Cognitive Assistance: From AI to Intelligence Amplification (IA)

A widely studied approach to increase the usefulness of crowdsourcing has been edge computing, which may be used to guide humans' step-by-step through the physical task execution process by providing them with *cognitive assistance*. Technically this could be easily realized by equipping humans with an augmented reality (AR) headset (e.g., HoloLens 2 with WiFi connectivity) that receives work-order information in real-time from its nearest AI-enhanced MEC server. Maier and Ebrahimzadeh [6] elaborated on the importance of shifting the research focus from AI to intelligence amplification (IA) by using information technology to enhance human decisions. Note, however, that IA becomes difficult in dynamic task environments of increased uncertainty and real-world situations of great complexity.

HITL Hybrid-Augmented Intelligence

Many problems that humans face tend to be of high uncertainty, complexity, and open-ended. To solve such problems, human interaction and participation must be introduced, giving rise to the concept of *HITL hybrid-augmented intelligence* for advanced human-machine collaboration. HITL hybrid-augmented intelligence is defined as an intelligent model that requires human interaction and allows for addressing problems and requirements that may not be easily trained or classified by machine learning. In general, machine learning is inferior to the human brain in understanding unstructured real-world environments and processing incomplete information and complex spatiotemporal correlation tasks. Hence, machines cannot carry out all the tasks in human society on their own. Instead, AI and human intelligence are better viewed as highly complementary.

The Internet provides an immense innovation space for HITL hybrid-augmented intelligence. Specifically, cloud robotics and AR are among the fastest-growing commercial applications for enhancing the intelligence of an individual in multi-robot collaborative systems. One of the main research topics of HITL hybrid-augmented intelligence is the development of methods that allow machines to learn from not only massive training samples but also human knowledge in order to accomplish highly intelligent tasks via shared intelligence among different robots and humans.

Decentralized Self-Organizing Cooperative (DSOC)

A very interesting example to catalyze human and machine intelligence toward a new form of self-organizing artificial general intelligence (AGI) across the Internet is the so-called *SingularityNET* (https://singularitynet.io). One can think of SingularityNet as a *decentralized self-organizing cooperative (DSOC)*, a concept similar to DAO. DSOC is essentially a distributed computing architecture for making new kinds of smart contracts. Entities executing these smart contracts are referred to as agents, which can run in the cloud, on phones, robots, or other embedded devices. Services are offered to any customer via APIs enabled by smart contracts and may require a combination of actions by multiple agents using their collective intelligence. In general, there may be multiple agents that can fulfill a given task request in different ways and to different degrees. Each task request to the network requires a unique combination of agents, thus forming a so-called *offer network* of mutual dependency, where agents make offers to each other to exchange services via offer-request pairs. Whenever someone wants an agent to perform services, a smart contract is signed for this specific task. Toward this end, DSOC aims at leveraging contributions from the broadest possible variety of agents by means of superior discovery mechanisms for finding useful agents and *nudging* them to become contributors.

Nudge Contract: Nudging via Smart Contract

Extending on DSOC and the judge contract introduced in the "Introduction" section, we develop a *nudge contract* for enhancing the human capabilities of unskilled crowd members of the DAO. According to Richard H. Thaler, the 2017 Nobel Laureate in Economics, a nudge is defined as any aspect of a choice architecture that alters people's behavior in a predictable way without forbidding any options or significantly changing their economic incentives. Deployed appropriately, nudges can *steer people*, as opposed to steer objects—real or virtual—as done in the conventional Tactile Internet, to make better choices and positively influence the behavior of crowds of all types.

Results

Our nudge contract aims at completing interrupted physical tasks by learning from a skilled DAO member with the objective of minimizing the learning loss, which denotes the difference between the achievable and optimum task execution times. Given the reward enabled by the nudge contract and associated with each skill transferred, a remote skilled DAO member submits a hash address of the learning instructions to an unskilled human/robot. The hash address is stored on the blockchain, whereby the corresponding data of the learning instructions may be stored on a remote decentralized storage server, e.g., Inter-Planetary File System (IPFS)[1]. An unskilled human/robot can retrieve the learning instructions using the corresponding hash address. The ability to learn a given subtask[2] is characterized by the subtask learning probability. The learning process is accomplished if each subtask is learned successfully from a skilled DAO member, who in turn is rewarded via a smart contract (see Algorithm 1 for details). Figure 3.4 shows the performance of our nudge contract for 50 DAO crowd members, whose ratio $\frac{f_{human}}{f_{robot}}$ is randomly chosen from {1/3, 3/3, 5/3}. We observe that for a given subtask learning probability, decreasing the number N_{sub} of subtasks helps reduce the

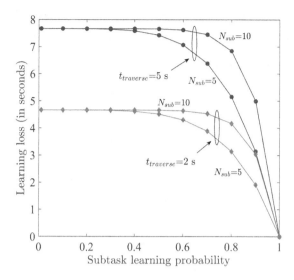

FIGURE 3.4 Learning loss (in seconds) vs. subtask learning probability for different number n_{sub} of subtasks and traverse time $t_{traverse}$.

learning loss, thus indicating the importance of a proper task decomposition method. More specifically, over-decomposition of the given task will result in performance deterioration unless a suitable learning mechanism is adopted to increase the subtask learning probability.

Algorithm 1 Nudge Contract

Input: Set $U = \{h_1, h_2, ..., h_n\}$ of n DAO members, capability vector $\mathbf{C} = [c_1, c_2, ..., c_n]$, distance vector $\mathbf{D} = [d_1, d_2, ..., d_n]$, interrupted task $\mathbf{T}$, required number D of actions to execute the interrupted task, interrupted robot r_0, capability requirement c_0 of the interrupted task

    1: Decompose the given interrupted task $\mathbf{T}$ into N_{sub} subtasks
    2: **for** $i = 1$ to n **do**
    3:   **if** $c_i \geq c_0$ **then**
    4:      $S \leftarrow h_i$
    5:   **end if**
    6: **end for**
    7: $h^* \leftarrow \arg \min_{d_i}\{S\}$
    8: Create a secure blockchain transaction between h^* and interrupted robot r_0
    9: Send the learning instructions from h^* to r_0 through the established transaction

10: Use the multi-arm bandit selection strategy in [8] to help the robot learn the given set of subtasks

11: **if** all N_{sub} subtasks are learned successfully **then**

12:    learning process is successfully accomplished

13:    r_0 can execute the interrupted task **T** with the capability of h^*

14: **else**

15:    Learning process is failed

16:    DAO member h^* traverses to the interruption point to execute the task **T**

17: **end if**

18: Reward the skilled DAO member h^* via blockchain smart contract

CONCLUSIONS

In this chapter, we explored how Ethereum blockchain technologies, in particular the DAO, may be leveraged to decentralize the Tactile Internet, which enables unprecedented mobile applications for remotely steering real or virtual objects/processes in perceived real-time and represents a promising example of future techno-social systems. We showed that a higher level of decentralization of AI-enhanced MEC reduces the average computational task completion time by up to 89.5% by setting the computation offloading probability to 0.7. Further, we observed that crowdsourcing of human assistance is beneficial in decreasing the average completion time of physical tasks for medium to high feedback misforecasting probabilities, provided the human offers equal or even superior operational capabilities, i.e., $\frac{f_{human}}{f_{robot}} \geq 1$. Toward this end, our proposed nudge contract tries to successfully accomplish tasks via shared intelligence among failing robots and skilled humans. An interesting research avenue to be explored is to offload the computation tasks not just on the MEC servers but also on the underutilized neighbor end-users, a method commonly known as *mobile ad hoc cloud*.

NOTES

1. https://ipfs.io/
2. We assume that the incoming physical tasks are decomposable, meaning that they can be broken into a number of subtasks. An example of such tasks can be the part assemblage in an industry automation scenario.

REFERENCES

1. T. M. Fernández-Caramés and P. Fraga-Lamas, "A Review on the Use of Blockchain for the Internet of Things," *IEEE Access*, vol. 6, pp. 32979–33001, May 2018.
2. Y. Zhang; S. Kasahara; Y. Shen; X. Jiang and J. Wan, "Smart Contract-Based Access Control for the Internet of Things," *IEEE Internet of Things Journal*, vol. 6, no. 2, pp. 1594–1605, April 2019.
3. R. Beck, "Beyond Bitcoin: The Rise of Blockchain World," *IEEE Computer*, vol. 51, no. 2, pp. 54–58, Feb. 2018.
4. A. McAfee and E. Brynjolfsson, *"Machine, Platform, Crowd: Harnessing Our Digital Future,"* W. W. Norton, New York, NY, USA, June 2017.
5. W. Saad; M. Bennis and M. Chen, "A Vision of 6G Wireless Systems: Applications, Trends, Technologies, and Open Research Problems," *IEEE Network*, vol. 34, no. 3, pp. 134–142, May/June 2020.
6. M. Maier and A. Ebrahimzadeh, "Towards Immersive Tactile Internet Experiences: Low-Latency FiWi Enhanced Mobile Networks with Edge Intelligence [Invited]," *IEEE/OSA Journal of Optical Communications and Networking, Special Issue on Latency in Edge Optical Networks*, vol. 11, no. 4, pp. B10–B25, Apr. 2019.
7. K. B. Letaief; W. Chen; Y. Shi; J. Zhang and Y. A. Zhang, "The Roadmap to 6G: AI Empowered Wireless Networks," *IEEE Communications Magazine*, vol. 57, no. 8, pp. 84–90, Aug. 2019.
8. S. McGuire; P. M. Furlong; C. Heckman; S. Julier; D. Szafir and N. Ahmed, "Failure is Not an Option: Policy Learning for Adaptive Recovery in Space Operations," *IEEE Robotics and Automation Letters*, vol. 3, no. 3, pp. 1639–1646, July 2018.

Blockchain Meets 6G

4

Social Human-Robot Interaction through Oracles and Behavioral Economics

---

INTRODUCTION

A major limitation of the conventional blockchain is its inability to interact with the "outside world" since smart contracts can only operate on data that is on the blockchain. In the emerging B-IoT, sensors are typically deployed to bring sensor measurement data onto the blockchain [1]. Advanced blockchain technologies enable the *on-chaining* of blockchain-external off-chain infor-mation stem-ming also from real users, apart from sensors and other data sources only, thus leveraging also on human intelligence rather than machine learning only. To overcome this limitation, smart contracts may make use of so-called *oracles*, which are trusted decentralized blockchain entities whose primary task is to collect off-chain information and bring it onto the block-chain as trustworthy input data to smart contracts. Several decentralized oracle systems exist that rely on *voting-based games*, e.g., ASTRAEA [2].

Blockchain-external data sources imply the risk that the on-chained data may be unreliable, maliciously modified, or untruthfully reported. Typically, various game-theoretical mechanisms are used to incentivize the

                                     DOI: 10.1201/9781003427322-4

truthful provisioning of data. According to Heiss et al. [3], however, those approaches address only partial aspects of the larger challenge of assuring *trustworthiness* in data on-chaining systems. A key property of trustworthy data on-chaining systems is truthfulness, which means that no execution of blockchain state transition is caused by untruthful data provisioning, but instead, data is always provisioned in a well-intended way. The challenge that derives from truthfulness is the building of incentive-compatible systems, where participants are assumed to act as rational self-interest driven *homini oeconomici*, whose primary goal is to maximize their individual utility via monetary rewards and penalties for their actions and behavior.

In this chapter, we focus on the *trust game* widely studied in behavioral economics. The trust game hasn't been investigated in a blockchain context yet, though it allows for a more systematic study of not only trust and trustworthiness but also reciprocity between human actors [4]. Next, we present a networked version of the trust game leveraging the beneficial characteristics of the social robots in changing players' behavior. Toward this end, we elaborate on the emerging field of *robonomics*, which studies the sociotechnical impact of blockchain technologies on social human-robot interaction. The classical trust game involves only two human players referred to as trustor and trustee, who are paired anonymously and are both endowed with a certain amount X of monetary units. Figure 4.1 illustrates the sequential exchange between trustor and trustee. The trustor can transfer a fraction $0 \leq p \leq 1$ of her/his endowment to the trustee. The experimenter then multiplies this amount by a factor $K > 1$, e.g., doubled or tripled. The trustee can transfer a fraction $0 \leq q \leq 1$ of the received amount directly back to the trustor

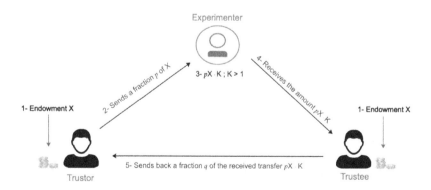

FIGURE 4.1 Classical trust game involving two human players (trustor and trustee) and one experimenter in the middle.

without going through the experimenter. Note that the trust game captures any generic economic exchange between two actors. According to Alós-Ferrer and Farolfi [5], the trust game will remain an important instrument for the study of social capital and its relation to economic growth for many years to come, whereby research on efficient cooperation and coordination technologies will be of particular interest.

The remainder of the chapter is structured as follows. In "6G Vision: Blockchains and Robots" section, we first briefly review the 6G vision of future mobile networks, followed by a discussion of the challenges and benefits of blockchain in 6G networks paying close attention to the anticipated role of blockchain oracles and persuasive robots. In "Blockchain-Enabled Trust Game" section, we identify open research challenges of realizing a blockchain-enabled trust game, including its social efficiency performance and the design of suitable reward and penalty mechanisms. We then delve into the technical issues of implementing a smart-contract-based decentralized version of the classical trust game by applying basic blockchain technologies and validating them experimentally. "On-Chaining Oracle for Networked N-Player Trust Game" section explores advanced blockchain technologies, most notably on-chaining oracles, to facilitate equitable social efficiency in a networked N-player (i.e., multiplayer) trust game. In "Robonomics: Playing the N-Player Trust Game with Persuasive Robots" section, we put the N-player trust game in the context of robonomics leveraging the beneficial characteristics of robot persuasive strategies to foster prosocial human behavior. Finally, "Conclusions" section concludes the chapter.

6G VISION: BLOCKCHAINS AND ROBOTS

Blockchain Benefits for 6G

Blockchain is used to generate the large-scale index as a security measure for all network communication. It serves as a mutual, collective, and common ledger. Blockchain performs the transition from client-server to a trusted peer-to-peer network. According to Saad et al. [6], blockchain and distributed ledger technology (DLT) may be viewed as the next generation of distributed sensing services, whose need for connectivity will require a synergistic mix of ultra-reliable and low-latency communications (URLLC) and massive machine-type communications (mMTC) to guarantee low-latency, reliable connectivity, and scalability [7]. A combination of blockchain technologies and sixth generation (6G) communications network yield the following benefits:

- **Intelligent Resource Management:** According to David and Berndt [8], network resource management and sharing play a significant role in 6G. Resource management operations such as spectrum sharing, orchestration, and decentralized computation have to be compatible with massive infrastructure volumes. Toward this end, blockchain and smart contracts are anticipated to play a major role for self-organizing network resource management. Further, smart contracts help handle and automate the relationship between operators and end-users.

- **Security and Privacy Features:** Another important benefit is the sophisticated use of all 6G network resources, services, and user data without compromising user security and privacy [8]. In this regard, security and privacy-preserving solutions based on blockchain such as decentralized authentication and access control, data ownership, integrity, traceability, and monitoring as well as the self-sovereign identity (SSI) paradigm, have been emerging to provide users with mechanisms that enable them to become anonymous, secure, and take control of their personal data during digital transactions.

- **Trustworthy 6G Communications:** 6G will fuse the digital and physical worlds for the purpose of sensing the real world and integrate far-reaching applications, ranging from autonomous systems to extended reality [8]. The opportunities for exploiting blockchain in 6G network infrastructures enhance the trustworthiness and performance gains of new services. For instance, blockchain can enable trusted charging and billing without centralized intermediaries. In addition, blockchain helps establish trusted and decentralized service level agreement (SLA) management given that, similar to 5G, 6G builds on virtualized and sliced network architectures. However, these solutions still need to be implemented at an extremely large scale. As a result, 6G is expected to support a very wide range of use cases with diverse SLA guarantees that need to be managed in a trusted manner.

Blockchains and Robots

Saad et al. [6] observed that the ongoing deployment of fifth generation (5G) cellular systems is exposing their inherent limitations compared to the original premise of 5G as an enabler for the Internet of Everything (IoE). They argue that 6G should not only explore more spectrum at high-frequency bands but, more importantly, converge driving technological trends. Among others, they claim that there will be the following three driving applications behind 6G: (*i*) blockchain and distributed ledger technologies, (*ii*) connected robotics and autonomous systems, and (*iii*) wireless brain-computer interaction (a subclass of human-machine interaction). In fact, in 6G, there is a strong notion that the nature of mobile terminals will change, whereby intelligent mobile robots are anticipated to play a more important role [7]. More specifically, David and Berndt [8] argue that 6G services that could provide human users with good advice would certainly be appreciated. According to the world's first 6G white paper published by the 6Genesis Flagship Program (6GFP) in September 2019, 6G will become more human-centered than 5G, which primarily focused on industry verticals.

This brief review of the 6G vision shows that blockchain technologies and robots are anticipated to play a central role in future mobile networks, which will become more human-centered than previous generations of cellular networks. Advanced blockchain technologies such as oracles that enable the on-chaining of blockchain-external off-chain information stemming from human users hold promise to leverage also on human intelligence rather than machine learning only. Similarly, intelligent mobile robots interacting with human users appear a promising solution to not only give physical and/or emotional assistance, but also to nudge human behavior by benefitting from persuasive robots.

BLOCKCHAIN-ENABLED TRUST GAME

In this section, we first identify open research challenges, then, we develop a blockchain-enabled implementation of the classical trust game using Ethereum and experimentally investigate the beneficial impact of a simple yet effective blockchain mechanism known as *deposit* on enhancing both trust and trustworthiness as well as increasing social efficiency.

Open Research Challenges

The use of decentralized blockchain technologies for the trust game should tackle the following research challenges:

- **Social Efficiency:** Recall from above that the trust game allows the study of social capital for achieving economic growth. Toward this end, the closely related term *social efficiency* plays an important role. Social efficiency is defined as the optimal distribution of resources in society, taking into account so-called externalities as well. In general, an externality is the cost or benefit that affects third parties other than the voluntary exchange between a pair of producer and consumer. We will study the impact of externalities below, when we extend the classical trust game to multiplayer games. We measure social efficiency as the ratio of the achieved total payoff of both trustor and trustee and the maximum achievable total payoff, which is equal to $X(K + 1)$. A social efficiency of 100% is achieved if the trustor sends her/his full endowment X (i.e., $p = 1$), which is then multiplied by K, and the trustee reciprocates by sending back the received amount XK fully or in part, translating into a total payoff of $q \cdot XK + (1 - q) \cdot XK + X = X(K + 1)$. Note that maximizing the total payoffs requires to set $p = 1$ for a given value of K, though q may be set to any arbitrary value. The parameter q, however, plays an important role in controlling the (equal or unequal) distribution of the total payoffs between trustor and trustee, as discussed in more detail shortly. Conversely, if the trustor decides to send nothing (i.e., $p = 0$) due to the lack of trust (on the trustor's side) and/or lack of trustworthiness (on the trustee's side), both are left with their endowment X and the social efficiency equals $2X/X(K + 1) = 2/(K + 1)$. How to improve social efficiency in an equitable fashion in a blockchain-enabled trust game is an important research challenge.

- **Trust and Trustworthiness in N-Player Trust Game:** In the past, games of trust have been limited to two players. Abbass et al. [9] introduced a new N-player trust game that generalizes the concept of trust, which is normally modeled as a sequential two-player game to a population of multiple players that can play the game concurrently. According to Abbass et al. [9] evolutionary game theory shows that a society with no untrustworthy individuals would yield maximum wealth to both the society as a whole and the individual in the long run. However, when the initial population consists of even the slightest number of untrustworthy individuals, the society converges to zero trustors. The proposed N-player trust game shows that the promotion of trust is an uneasy task, despite the fact that a combination of trustors and trustworthy trustees is the most rational and optimal social state.

It's important to note that the N-player trust game in [9] was played in an unstructured environment, i.e., the population was not structured in any specific spatial topology or social network. Chica et al. [10] investigated whether a *networked* version of the N-player trust game would promote higher levels of trust and global net wealth (i.e., total payoffs) in the population than that of an unstructured population. To do so, players were mapped to a spatial network structure, which restricts their interactions and cooperation with local neighborhoods. Unlike Abbas et al. [9], where the existence of a single untrustworthy individual would eliminate trust completely and lead to zero global net wealth, Chica et al. [10] discovered the importance of establishing network structures for promoting trust and global net wealth in the N-player trust game in that trust can be promoted despite a substantial number of untrustworthy individuals in the initial population. Clearly, the development of appropriate communication network solutions for achieving efficient cooperation and coordination among players with different strategies in a networked N-player trust game represents an interesting research challenge.

- **Reward & Penalty Mechanism Design:** For the implementation of desirable social goals, the theory of *mechanism design* plays an important role. According to Maskin [11], the theory of mechanism design can be thought of as the "engineering" side of economic theory. While the economic theorist wants to explain or forecast the social outcomes of mechanisms, the mechanism design theory reverses the direction of inquiry by identifying first the social goal and then asking whether or not an appropriate mechanism could be designed to attain that goal. And if the answer is yes, what form that mechanism might take, whereby a mechanism may be an institution, procedure, or game for determining desirable outcomes.

  An interesting example of mechanism design is the so-called *altruistic punishment* to ensure human cooperation in multiplayer public goods games [12]. Altruistic punishment means that individuals punish others, even though the punishment is costly and yields no material gain. It was experimentally shown that altruistic punishment of defectors (i.e., untrustworthy participants) is a key motive for cooperation in that cooperation flourishes if altruistic punishment is possible, and breaks down if it is ruled out. The design of externalities such as third-party punishment and alternative reward mechanisms for incentivizing human cooperation in multiplayer public goods games in general and N-player trust game in particular is of great importance.

- **Decentralized Implementation of Economic Experiments:** A widely used experimental software for developing and conducting almost any kind of economic experiments, including the aforementioned public goods games and our considered trust game, is the *Zurich Toolbox for Ready-made Economics (z-Tree)* [13]. *The* z-Tree software is implemented as a client-server application with a central server application for the experimenter, called z-Tree, and a remote client application for the game participants, called z-Leaf. It is available free of charge and allows economic experiments to be conducted via the Internet. On the downside, however, z-Tree does not support peer-to-peer (P2P) communications between players, as opposed to a decentralized blockchain-enabled implementation.

Experimenter Smart Contract

First, we develop a smart contract that replaces the experimenter in the middle between trustor and trustee (see Fig. 4.1). The development process makes use of the Truffle framework[1], a decentralized application development framework. The resultant experimenter smart contract is written in the programming language Solidity. We then compile the experimenter smart contract into Ethereum EVM byte code. Once the experimenter smart contract is compiled, it generates the EVM byte code and Application Binary Interface (ABI). Next, we deploy the experimenter smart contract on Ethereum's official test network Ropsten. It can be invoked by using its address and ABI.

More specifically, in our experimenter contract, we use the following global variables: (*i*) *msg.value*, which represents the transaction that is sent, and (*ii*) *msg.sender*, which represents the address of the player who has sent the transaction to the experimenter smart contract, i.e., trustor or trustee. Both trustor and trustee use their Ethereum Externally Owned Account (EOA), which uses public and private keys to interact and invoke each function of our experimenter smart contract. In the following, we provide a brief overview of the core functions and parameters of our experimenter smart contract:

- **Function investFraction():** This function allows the trustor to invest a portion p of her endowment X. Once called, it takes the received msg.value p from the trustor, multiplies it by factor K using the contract balance, and transfers it directly to the trustee's account. The trustee receives *msg.value* $\cdot K$.
- **Function splitFraction():** This function allows the trustee to split a portion q of the received investment from the trustor. Once called, it takes the set split amount from the trustee's account and sends it to the trustor's account.
- **Parameter Onlytrustor (modifier type):** This modifier is applied to the *investFraction()* function. Thus, only the trustor can invoke this function of the experimenter smart contract.

- **Parameter Onlytrustee (modifier type):** This modifier is applied to the *splitFraction()* function. Thus, only the trustee can invoke this function of the experimenter smart contract.

We note that after the execution of each function of the experimenter smart contract, an event is used to create notifications and saved logs. Events help trace and notify both players about the current state of the contract and activities.

Blockchain Mechanism Deposit

The use of one-way security deposits to provide trust for one party with respect to the other is quite common, particularly for the exchange of goods and services via e-commerce and crowdsourcing platforms. In the context of blockchains, a deposit is an agreement smart contract that defines the arrangement between parties, where one party deposits an asset with a third party. An interesting use case of the blockchain mechanism deposit can be found in [14]. In this paper, the authors propose a new protocol that achieves the fulfillment of all the desired properties of a registered electronic Delivery (e-Deliveries) service using blockchain. In the proposed protocol, the authors included a deposit mechanism with the aim to encourage the sender to avoid dishonest behavior and fraud attempts, and also to conclude the exchange in a predefined way following the phases of the protocol. The deposit will be returned to the sender if he finishes the exchange according to the protocol. In our work, we propose to add an optional function *deposit()* to our experimenter smart contract to improve trust and trustworthiness between both players. Toward this end, we make the following two modifications:

- **Function deposit():** This function allows the trustee to submit an amount of $2 \leq D \leq X$ monetary units (i.e., Ether in our considered case of Ethereum) as a deposit to the experimenter smart contract. The deposit is returned to the trustee only if a transaction with $q > 0$ is completed. Otherwise, with $q = 0$, the trustee loses the deposit. It should be noted that the aforementioned *Onlytrustee()* modifier is also applied to this function.
- **Function splitFraction():** We make a modification to this function to allow the trustee to split the received amount (i.e., $q > 0$). Otherwise, the transaction is rejected until the trustee splits the received amount. Once this happens, the function transfers the amount to the trustor's account and returns the deposit D to the trustee's account.

Experimental Setup

Next, we investigate the impact of the deposit as an effective pre-commitment mechanism on the trust game performance (i.e., social efficiency and normalized reciprocity) via Ethereum-based blockchain experiments. We set $K = 2$ in our experimenter smart contract and consider different deposit values of $D = \{0, 2, 5, X\}$ Ether, whereby $D = 0$ denotes the classical trust game without any deposit. The experiment was conducted with two graduate students from different universities. The rationale behind the selection of only two students is to first focus on the conventional trust game that by definition involves only two players. This allows us to be more certain that the effects of the deposit mechanism are real. In addition, conducting our experiment with the same two participating students allows us to better observe the behavior change during the rounds of the game. As for our inclusion criteria, we note that the students didn't know each other's identity, which was important to ensure anonymity between them. Further, the students hadn't conducted any behavioral research experiments before. Nor did either participant had any prior knowledge or experience with the trust game or any other investment game experiments. The two participating students were male and their age was 23 and 25 years, respectively.

At the beginning of the experiment, both trustor and trustee were given an endowment of $X = 10$ Ether. We ran the experiment four times, each time for a different value of D. Each of the four experiments took five rounds. We note that for the experiment with $D = 10$ Ether, the trustee put her full endowment X into the deposit, thus $D = X$ Ether. All experiments were run across the Internet. Both participants interacted with our experimenter's smart contract using their Ethereum accounts. We note that both the trustor and the trustee need to pay a gas fee. Gas price refers to the pricing value, required to successfully conduct a transaction or execute a function in a smart contract on the Ethereum blockchain platform. Priced in small fractions of the cryptocurrency Ether, commonly referred to as Gwei. Each Gwei is equal to 0.000000001 ETH (10^{-9} Ether). Given its lowest cost, we considered transaction fees associated with deploying the smart contract and sending transactions negligible compared to the amounts invested and split.

Results

Figure 4.2 depicts the average social efficiency and normalized reciprocity (both given in percent) vs. deposit $D = \{0, 2, 5, X\}$ (given in Ether). We define normalized reciprocity as the ratio of q/p as a measure of the trustee's reciprocity, q, in response to the trustor's generosity, p. Note that the normalized reciprocity is useful to gauge the fair distribution of total payoffs from trustee

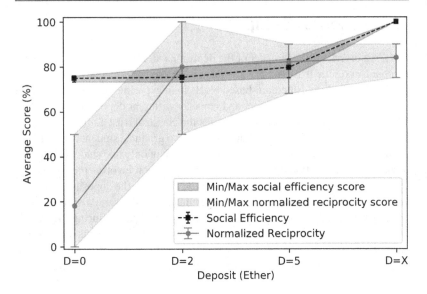

FIGURE 4.2   Average social efficiency and normalized reciprocity q/p vs. deposit $d = \{0, 2, 5, x\}$ ether using experimenter smart contract with $k = 2$ and $x = 10$ (shown with minimum-to-maximum measured score intervals).

to trustor, and vice versa, for a given achievable social efficiency. Note that Fig. 4.2 also shows the interval between minimum and maximum measured score for each value of D.

We make the following interesting observations from Fig. 4.2. First, the social efficiency continually grows for an increasing deposit D until it reaches the maximum of 100% for $D = X$. Thus, the social efficiency performance of the classical trust game can be maximized by applying the blockchain chain mechanism of deposit properly with $D = X$. This is due to the fact that the trustor sends her full endowment (i.e., $p = 1$) after the trustee has put in her maximum deposit. In doing so, a maximum total payoff of 30 Ether is achieved, translating into a social efficiency of 100%. It is worthwhile to mention that this was the case in all five rounds of the experiment. Second, the average normalized reciprocity improves significantly for increasing deposit D compared to the classical trust game without any deposit ($D = 0$).

Specifically, in the classical trust game, the average normalized reciprocity is as low as 18%. By contrast, for a deposit of as little as $D = 2$ Ether, the average normalized reciprocity rises to 80%. Interestingly, further increasing D does not lead to sizeable additional increases, e.g., average normalized reciprocity equals 83% for $D = X$. Hence, the amount of the deposit does not change the normalized reciprocity significantly with $q/p \approx 80\%$ for $D > 0$. Finally, Fig. 4.2 illustrates that for an increasing deposit D, the behavior of the two players becomes more consistent, as indicated by the decreasing intervals of minimum to maximum measured scores.

In the subsequent section, we extend the classical two-player trust game to a networked N-player trust game and study how advanced blockchain technologies, most notably on-chaining oracles, drive the behavior of players by means of different reward and penalty mechanisms. Among others, we seek to understand whether an increased normalized reciprocity is achievable without sacrificing social efficiency.

ON-CHAINING ORACLE FOR NETWORKED *N*-PLAYER TRUST GAME

Architecture of Oracle

Figure 4.3 depicts the architecture of our proposed on-chaining oracle for the networked N-player trust game. The proposed architecture comprises a set of clusters or pools. Each cluster contains three types of agents: (*i*) trustors, (*ii*) trustees, and (*iii*) observers. The difference between observers and players (trustors/trustees) is that observers don't play, but track and evaluate trust and trustworthiness criteria such as investment (p) and split (q). Players interact with the experimenter smart contract using their public-private keys through a DApp. The different rounds of the game are monitored remotely by the observers using *Etherscan*[2], an Ethereum blockchain explorer that uses the experimenter contract address and shows the different transactions between each pair of trustor and trustee in real-time. We note that alternatively, one may use *Alethio*[3], a monitoring tool that allows observers to send and receive alerts to and from any on-chain address, activity, or function.

The design of a third-party punishment and reward mechanism for incentivizing player cooperation in our networked N-player trust game is based on crowdsourcing. Specifically, observers provide their collective human intelligence to the nudge contract in order to punish a cluster or an individual player, who demonstrates inappropriate behavior, or provide a positive reward for good behavior. The nudge contract manages the reward-penalty mechanism in the form of loyalty points. A trustor can earn loyalty points for an honest transaction, investment, and engagement in the game and redeem earned points for rewards. Similarly, the trustee is rewarded for generous reciprocity. Loyalty points keep the players engaged and aware of the overall goals, i.e., increase of total payoff, social efficiency, and normalized reciprocity. In addition, the players have a score profile associated with their public key, whereby

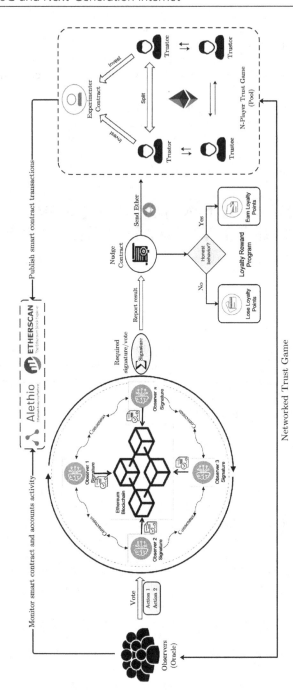

FIGURE 4.3   Architecture of on-chaining oracle for networked *n*-player trust game.

players earn 1 point for every honest action and lose 1 point if their action is dishonest. The scoring profile is managed by the nudge contract. Trustor and trustee can check the status of their loyalty reward points by calling the function *getTrustorLoyalty*() and *getTrusteeLoyalty*(), respectively. Furthermore, an incentive strategy was designed to incorporate principles of behavioral psychology using economic outcomes to render the system more effective in changing the players' behavior. Players earn a monetary reward in the form of Ether after reaching a certain number of loyalty reward points in the game, e.g., 10 points = 1 Ether.

The ethers earned are added to the player's endowment X, which will be used for the investment and payoff in future rounds of the game. We note that there are more advanced schemes to compute the score/reputation of users, e.g., [15, 16].

On-Chaining of Voting-Based Decisions

In our oracle implementation, we assigned predetermined public keys to both players and observers. The creation of each key pair can be accomplished by using several options, including Ethereum wallets and online/offline Ethereum address generators, e.g., Vanity-ETH [4]. All public keys are declared in the nudge contract, whose purpose is to allow only registered observers to vote while automatically rejecting malicious voters. To facilitate the formation of a majority, the number of possible voting options is restricted to the four following functions on the nudge contract: *VOTE_RewardTrustor*, *VOTE_RewardTrustee*, *VOTE_PunishTrustor*, and *VOTE_PunishTrustee*. Recall that a function is a code that resides at a specific smart contract address on the Ethereum blockchain. Further, to ensure a trustworthy on-chaining decision, a k-out-of-M threshold signature is used to reach a consensus on the function to be executed. A k-out-of-M threshold signature scheme is a protocol that allows any subset of k players out of M players to generate a signature, and disallows the creation of a valid signature if fewer than k players should participate. The right decision is determined as the one that has received the desired number of votes. Once the function is executed, the nudge contract allocates the reward or punishment loyalty points to each player who behaved in a trusted or untrusted way, respectively.

Results

We compare the performance of our proposed on-chaining oracle for the multiplayer N-player trust game with the conventional two-player baseline experiment. Toward this end, we invited the same two students, who have played the classical two-player trust game before, and asked them to play the game again, i.e., without any observers. Next, we invited them to play the game in the presence of two observers. The two players were informed that their account is associated with loyalty reward points, which will be increased if they act honestly. Otherwise, they will be punished and lose 1 loyalty point. Both players were aware that they will be rewarded with 1 Ether for each 10 accumulated loyalty reward points. In addition, they are notified that the decision will be made by two observers, who will monitor their online transactions in order to make their independent reward/penalty decisions. All four participants interact anonymously via the Internet.

Figure 4.4 compares the average social efficiency of the two-player trust game without observers with that of the four-player trust game with observers. The figure clearly demonstrates the beneficial impact of the presence of observers on social efficiency for all values of D. Note that with observers the instantaneous social efficiency reaches the maximum of 100% for all values of D, as opposed to the two-player trust game where this occurs requiring the full deposit of $D = X$ Ether. As for the normalized reciprocity achievable with and without observers, things are similar, as shown in Fig. 4.5. However,

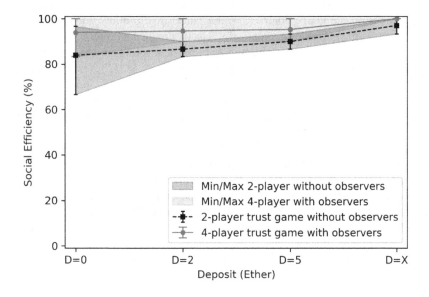

FIGURE 4.4 Average social efficiency vs. deposit $d = \{0, 2, 5, x\}$ ether for two-player trust game without observers and 4-player trust game with observers (shown with minimum-to-maximum measured score intervals).

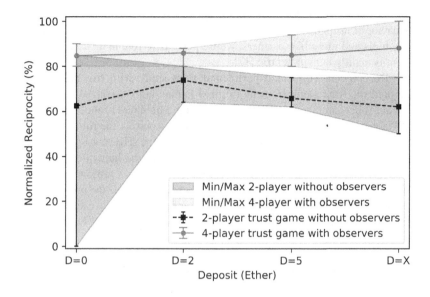

FIGURE 4.5 Average normalized reciprocity q/p vs. deposit $d = \{0, 2, 5, x\}$ ether for two-player trust game without observers and 4-player trust game with observers (shown with minimum-to-maximum measured score intervals).

while the presence of observers helps raise the average (and instantaneous) normalized reciprocity consistently above 80% (compared to below 80% in Fig. 4.2), there still remains room for further improvement, especially for $0 \le D < X$.

ROBONOMICS: PLAYING THE *N*-PLAYER TRUST GAME WITH PERSUASIVE ROBOTS

Robonomics: Key Principles

Many studies have shown that the physical presence of robots benefits a variety of social interaction elements such as persuasion, likeability, and trustworthiness. Thus, leveraging these beneficial characteristics of social robots represents a promising solution toward enhancing the performance of the trust game. Social robots connected with human operators form a physical embodiment that creates the new paradigm of an immersive coexistence between humans and robots, whereby persuasive robots aim at changing the behavior of users through social influence. Importantly, these robots are less like tools and more like partners, whose persuasive role in a social environment is mainly human-centric [17].

Recently, in [18], an experimental pilot study with five participants adapted the trust game from its original human-human context to a social human-robot interaction (sHRI) setting using a humanoid robot operated in a *Wizard-of-Oz (WoZ)* manner, where a person controls the robot remotely. The obtained findings suggest that people playing the sHRI trust game follow a human-robot trust model that is quite similar to the human-human trust model. However, due to the lack of common *social cues* present in humans (e.g., facial expressions or gestures) that generally influence the initial assessment of trustworthiness, almost all participants started investing a lower amount and increased it after actively exploring the robot's behavior and trustworthiness through social experience.

In the following, we focus on the emerging field of *robonomics*, which studies the sociotechnical impact of blockchain technologies on sHRI, behavioral economics, behavioral game theory, and cryptocurrencies (both coins and tokens) for the social integration of robots into human society [19]. Robonomics involves persuasive robotics, whereby a physical or virtual robotic agent is used as enforcer or supervisor of human behavior modification via psychological rewards in addition to tangible rewards. In a recent exploratory sHRI study [20], ten multimodal *persuasive strategies* were compared with regard to their effectiveness of social robots attempting to influence human behavior. It was experimentally shown that two particular persuasive strategies—affective and logical strategies—achieved the highest persuasiveness and trustworthiness.

Persuasive Robotics Strategies

Similar to [21], we developed a *Crowd-of-Oz (CoZ)* platform for letting observers remotely control the gestures of Softbank's social robot Pepper placed in front of the trustee and have a real-time dialogue via web-based text-to-speech translation. The CoZ user interface is built using a Django web server. The trustee can communicate with Pepper through voice and Pepper's tactile tablet. To support voice communication, we implemented a web-based speech-to-text tool. When text is extracted from voice, the trustee can see his/her message on Pepper's tablet in order to verify it. Next, the speech-to-text function calls another function to add additional fields to the main message (extracted text), including sequence ID, sender ID, message type, and time to make the message distinguishable on the Django server. The called function executes a marshaling process and sends the message to the Django server through the OOCSI middleware[5]. The OOCSI middleware is a message-based connectivity layer and is platform-independent inspired by the concept of RPC (Remote Procedure Call) for connecting web clients.

In our developed CoZ system, there are two types of messages: information and control. The information messages are created by the observers. This type of message is multicast to all observers and the trustee through Pepper to update them, but not the trustor. The trustee can see all the information messages on Pepper's tablet. Moreover, Pepper uses a text-to-speech function to transfer the observers' messages to the trustee. The control messages are used for important functionalities of the CoZ architecture, e.g., performing a gesture on Pepper. When an observer presses a social cue button, the CoZ web-interface invokes a JavaScript method to call a new event on the Django server. The invoked method sets all the related joints' angles plus the Light-Emitting Diode (LED) colors of Pepper's eyes. Given that two or more observers may press the same or different social cue buttons simultaneously, the Django server implemented a queue to synchronize all issued commands. While Pepper is performing a gesture, the Django server puts the next gesture in the queue and sends it to Pepper back-to-back.

Further, our CoZ user interface provides a section, where an observer can watch the trustee's environment through Pepper's eyes. To implement this part, we used OpenCV[6], Flask[7], and CV2[8] tools. The Django server invokes a method on Pepper called "ALVideoDevice" to start recording videos. Next, the Flask server stores the sequence of produced videos with a valid Uniform Resource Locator (URL). To make live video streams accessible over the Internet we used Virtual Private Network (VPN). Moreover, in our CoZ interface, we used an IFrame (Inline Frame) tag to demonstrate live video streaming using a valid URL. An IFrame is an HyperText Markup Language (HTML) document embedded inside another HTML document on a website. The IFrame HTML element is often used to insert content from another source, such as a camera, into a Web page. In our CoZ user interface, we also realized four buttons to turn Pepper's head to the left, right, up, and down. When an observer presses one of these buttons, the CoZ interface invokes a method to create a control message, marshaling process, and send it to the Django server. Upon reception, the Django server performs unmarshaling to extract the main message and then invokes the "ALMotion" along with initializing some parameters like speed, angle, and joint name. For each invocation, Pepper turns her head by ten degrees.

The user CoZ interface also displays nine social cue buttons to prevent possible typos and save time for observers to fill communication gaps. The nine social cue buttons were as follows: "Gain time," "Tell me about it," "Good job," "Hi," "Bye," "Open arms," "Taunting hands," "No," and "Ask for attention." Observers may press to perform different gestures of Pepper during conversation and thereby influence the trustee's behavior. In addition, we drafted two scripts, one for a logical persuasive strategy appealing to the left side of the brain (i.e., logics) and another one for an affective persuasive strategy appealing to the right side of the brain (i.e., emotions) of the trustee. Each script contains pre-specified sentences stored in pull-down menus in the CoZ interface, from which observers may choose in order to nudge the trustee's behavior toward reciprocity via real-time text-to-speech messages. The different persuasive robot strategies operate as follows:

- **Logical Strategy**: Contains a set of reward and punishment mechanisms. In addition, Pepper performs some economical and technical advice via text-to-speech through the above described CoZ platform.
- **Affective Strategy**: Contains a set of reward/punishment mechanisms and Pepper uses text-to-speech encouragement messages through the CoZ platform. In addition, Pepper shows social cues by means of gestures and embodied communications toward the trustee.
- **Mixed Strategy**: Combines the above logical and affective strategies into one mixed strategy. It contains a set of reward/punishment mechanisms and Pepper provides not only economical and technical advice but also encouragement via text-to-speech messages through the CoZ platform. In addition, Pepper shows social cues by means of gestures and embodied communications toward the trustee.

For illustration, Table 4.1 lists the social cues used by Pepper in our proposed mixed logical-affective persuasive strategy. In this strategy, one observer plays the logical strategy and the other observer plays the affective strategy such that the trustee receives mixed messages and mixed-em-bodied communications. Depending on the trustee's behavior, the observers carry out the "Trusted behavior action" or the "Untrusted behavior action" in each round of the experiment. The social cues in Table 4.1 enable the observers to control Pepper's text-to-speech and embodied communications using our developed CoZ platform.

Experimental Setup

We ran large-scale experiments involving 20 students to measure the effectiveness of our developed persuasive robotics strategies (i.e., logical, affective, and mixed strategies). Similar to our last experiment in the two players' trust game, the participating students didn't know each other's identity. Also, students

TABLE 4.1   Social cues used by Pepper in mixed persuasive strategy

ROUND NUMBER	TRUSTED BEHAVIOR ACTION	UNTRUSTED BEHAVIOR ACTION
Round 1	*Text-to-speech:* Trust Game is a cooperative investment game. You all play together to get the best total payoff!	Untrusted behavior will be shown in Round 2
Round 2	*Text-to-speech:* Awesome! That's a split worth celebrating! *Embodied communication:* Open arm gesture.	*Text-to-speech:* If this behavior is repeated, you will receive a punishment from the observers. *Embodied communication:* Taunting hand gesture.
Round 3	*Text-to-speech:* If this good behavior is repeated, your partner will invest more in the next round. *Embodied communication:* Open arm gesture.	*Text-to-speech:* Weak reciprocity can cause costly punishment for you. *Embodied communication:* Taunting hand gesture.
Round 4	*Text-to-speech:* Incredible! Your partner must be impressed! *Embodied communication:* Open arm gesture.	*Text-to-speech:* With such a behavior, the punishment will be executed next round. *Embodied communication:* Taunting hand gesture.
Round 5	*Text-to-speech:* Congrats! Your good behavior toward your partner has provided you with an incremental total payoff over all rounds of the game. *Embodied communication:* Open arm gesture.	*Text-to-speech:* Your bad behavior translated into a very weak total payoff. *Embodied communication:* Taunting hand gesture.

hadn't conducted any behavioral research experiments before. The age of the selected students was between 24 and 32 years. Three students were female and seventeen students were male. The experiment was divided into four trials: baseline, logical, affective, and mixed strategy. Each trial involved 5 rounds. We first conducted a baseline trust-game experiment, where trustees didn't interact with Pepper, as done previously, followed by experiments exposing trustees to Pepper's logical, affective, and mixed logical-affective persuasive strategies. Both trustor and trustee interacted via a blockchain account with the experimenter's smart contract. The trustor played the game from a separate room, while the trustee was in the lab alone with Pepper. Pepper was controlled via our CoZ platform remotely by the observer. We used the same parameter settings, i.e., endowment $X = 10$ Ether for the trustor and $K = 2$. Further, in all persuasive strategies, we didn't use any deposit mechanism (i.e., $D = 0$).

Results

Figure 4.6 demonstrates the superior effectiveness of our persuasive strategies, especially mixed ones appealing to both sides of the brain, resulting in average normalized reciprocity well above 100%. Further, to better reveal the differences among the persuasive strategies, we have calculated the measurement range for the four strategies. The measurement range for the baseline

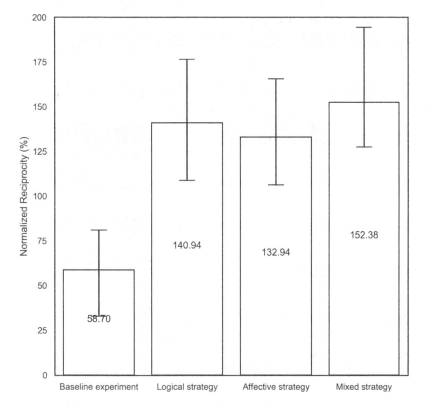

FIGURE 4.6 Average normalized reciprocity q/p without (baseline experiment) and with using logical, affective, and mixed logical-affective persuasive strategies for $d = 0$ (shown with minimum-to-maximum measured score intervals).

experiment is 48.2 (Max = 81, Min = 32.8), while for the logical strategy, it is 67.8 (Max = 176.4, Min = 108.6), for the affective strategy, it is 59.4 (Max = 165.6, Min = 106.2), and the mixed strategy, it is 67 (Max = 194.4, Min = 127.4). As the results show, the baseline experiment has the smallest measurement range. Next, we computed the standard deviation for the baseline experiment as well as logical, affective, and mixed strategies, which is equal to 15.6, 21.75, 21.10, and 22.73, respectively. The results show that the baseline experiment has the smallest standard deviation among all considered strategies, while the mixed strategy has the largest one. Finally, we have computed the variance for the persuasive strategies under consideration. The calculated variance equals 245.83, 473.17, 445.25, and 517.03 for the baseline, logical, affective, and mixed strategy, respectively. Based on the gathered results, we observe that the baseline experiment has the smallest and the mixed strategy has the largest variance.

CONCLUSIONS

Robonomics is a recently emerging sociotechnical field of interdisciplinary research that integrates behavioral economics with advanced blockchain technologies and persuasive robotics. Given its prominent role in behavioral economics and the relevance of trust in blockchains, we focused on the trust game, including its networked multiplayer extension. We experimentally demonstrated the beneficial impact of the blockchain mechanisms deposit and on-chaining oracle on improving both social efficiency and reciprocity significantly. Our experimental results show that the presence of third parties such as human observers and in particular social robots play an important role in a blockchain-enabled trust game. While the trust game's central experimenter may be easily replaced with our presented experimenter smart contract, the peer pressure executed by on-chaining oracles and especially the embodied communications enabled by persuasive robots were shown to have a potentially greater social impact than monetary incentives such as deposit, opening up new research avenues for future work.

NOTES

1. https://www.trufflesuite.com/
2. https://etherscan.io

3. https://reports.aleth.io/
4. https://vanity-eth.tk/
5. https://oocsi.id.tue.nl/
6. https://opencv.org/
7. https://flask.palletsprojects.com/en/2.0.x/
8. https://pypi.org/project/opencv-python/

REFERENCES

1. O. Novo, "Blockchain Meets IoT: An Architecture for Scalable Access Management in IoT," *IEEE Internet of Things Journal*, vol. 5, no. 2, pp. 1184–1195, April 2018.
2. J. Adler; R. Berryhill; A. Veneris; Z. Poulos; N. Veira and A. Kastania, "ASTRAEA: A Decentralized Blockchain Oracle," *Proceeding of IEEE International Conference on Cyber, Physical and Social Computing*, Halifax, NS, Canada, pp. 1145–1152, July/Aug. 2018.
3. J. Heiss; J. Eberhardt and S. Tai, "From Oracles to Trustworthy Data On-chaining Systems," *Proceedings of IEEE International Conference on Blockchain*, Atlanta, GA, USA, pp. 496–503, July 2019.
4. J. Berg; J. Dickhaut and K. McGabe, "Trust, Reciprocity, and Social History," *Games and Economic Behavior*, vol. 10, no. 1, pp. 122–142, July 1995.
5. C. Alós-Ferrer and F. Farolfi. "Trust Games and Beyond," *Frontiers in Neuroscience*, vol. 13, Article 887, pp. 1–14, Sep. 2019.
6. W. Saad; M. Bennis and M. Chen, "A Vision of 6G Wireless Systems: Applications, Trends, Technologies, and Open Research Problems," *IEEE Network*, vol. 34, no. 3, pp. 134–142, May/June 2020.
7. B. Zong; C. Fan; X. Wang; X. Duan; B. Wang and J. Wang, "6G Technologies: Key Drivers, Core Requirements, System Architectures, and Enabling Technologies," *IEEE Vehicular Technology Magazine*, vol. 14, no. 3, pp. 18–27, Sep. 2019.
8. K. David and H. Berndt, "6G Vision and Requirements: Is There Any Need for Beyond 5G?," *IEEE Vehicular Technology Magazine*, vol. 13, no. 3, pp. 72–80, Sep. 2018.
9. H. Abbass; G. Greenwood and E. Petraki, "The N-Player Trust Game and its Replicator Dynamics," *IEEE Transactions on Evolutionary Computation*, vol. 20, no. 3, pp. 470–474, June 2016.
10. M. Chica; R. Chiong; M. Kirley and H. Ishibuchi, "A Networked N-Player Trust Game and Its Evolutionary Dynamics," *IEEE Transactions on Evolutionary Computation*, vol. 22, no. 6, pp. 866–878, Dec. 2018.
11. E. S. Maskin, "Mechanism Design: How to Implement Social Goals," *The American Economic Review*, vol. 98, no. 3, pp. 567–576, June 2008.
12. E. Fehr and S. Gächter, "Altruistic Punishment in Humans," *Nature*, vol. 415, pp. 137–140, Jan. 2002.
13. U. Fischbacher, "z-Tree: Zurich toolbox for ready-made economic experiments," *Experimental Economics*, vol. 10, no. 2, pp. 171–178, June 2007.

14. M. Mut-Puigserver; M. A. Cabot-Nadal and M. M. Payeras-Capella, "Removing the Trusted Third Party in a Confidential Multiparty Registered eDelivery Protocol Using Blockchain," *IEEE Access*, vol. 8, pp. 106855–106871, June 2020.

15. M. Li; L. Zhu; Z. Zhang; C. Lal; M. Conti and M. Alazab, "Anonymous and Verifiable Reputation System for E-Commerce Platforms Based on Blockchain," *IEEE Transactions on Network and Service Management*, vol. 18, no. 4, pp. 4434–4449, Dec. 2021.

16. G. Fortino; F. Messina; D. Rosaci and M. L. Sarné, "Using Blockchain in a Reputation-Based Model for Grouping Agents in the Internet of Things," *IEEE Transactions on Engineering Management*, vol. 67, no. 4, pp. 1231–1243, Nov. 2020.

17. M. Siegel; C. Breazeal and M. I. Norton, "Persuasive Robotics: The Influence of Robot Gen-der on Human Behavior," *Proceedings of IEEE/RSJ International Conference on Intelligent Robots and Systems*, pp. 2563–2568, St. Louis, MO, USA, Oct. 2009.

18. R. C. R. Mota; D. J. Rea; A. L. Tran; J. E. Young; E. Sharlin and M. C. Sousa, "Playing the 'Trust Game' with Robots: Social Strategies and Experiences," *Proceedings of IEEE International Symposium on Robot and Human Interactive Communication*, pp. 519–524, New York City, NY, USA, Aug. 2016.

19. I. S. Cardenas and J.-H Kim, "Robonomics: The Study of Robot-Human Peer-to-Peer Financial Transactions and Agreements," *Proceedings of HRI '20: Companion of the 2020 ACM/IEEE International Conference on Human-Robot Interaction*, pp. 8–15, Cambridge, UK, March 2020.

20. S. Saunderson and G. Nejat, "It Would Make Me Happy if You Used My Guess: Comparing Robot Persuasive Strategies in Social Human-Robot Interaction," *IEEE Robotics and Automation Letters*, vol. 4, no. 2, pp. 1707–1714, April 2019.

21. T. Abbas; V.-J. Khan and P. Markopoulos, "CoZ: A Crowd-powered System for Social Robotics," *Elsevier SoftwareX*, vol. 11, 100421, pp. 1–7, Jan–June 2020.

From Superorganism to Stigmergic Society & Collective Intelligence in the 6G Era

5

INTRODUCTION

Unlike previous generations, future sixth generation (6G) networks are anticipated to be transformative by revolutionizing the wireless evolution from "connected things" to "connected intelligence" [1]. In his critically acclaimed book "Social Physics," a term originally coined by Auguste Comte, the founder of modern sociology, MIT Media Lab professor Alex Pentland argues that social interactions (e.g., social learning and social pressure) are the primary forces driving the evolution of *collective intelligence (CI)*. According to Pentland, CI emerges through shared learning of surrounding peers and harnessing the power of exposure to cause desirable behavior change and build communities. He concludes that humans have more in common with bees than we like to admit and that future techno-social systems should scale up ancient decision-making processes we see in bees.

DOI: 10.1201/9781003427322-5

This conclusion is echoed by Max Borders through his concept of the *social singularity* that defines the point beyond which humanity will operate much like a hive mind, i.e., CI. Currently, two separate processes are racing forward in time: (*i*) the technological singularity: Machines are getting smarter (e.g., machine learning and AI), and (*ii*) the social singularity: Humans are getting smarter. In fact, he argues that these two separate processes are two aspects of the same underlying process waiting to be woven together toward creating new *human-centric* industries. More and more, we'll act like bees to get big things done, whereby humans act as neurons in a human hive mind with blockchain technology acting as connective tissue to create virtual pheromone trails, i.e., programmable incentives.

Ever since the beginning of industrialization, three industrial revolutions have been experienced with the development of steam engines (mid-18–19th century), electrification (1870 onward), and digitization (1970 onward), respectively. The current fourth industrial revolution has been enabled through the Internet of Things (IoT) in association with other emerging technologies, most notably cyber-physical systems (CPS). CPS help bridge the gap between manufacturing and information technologies and give birth to the smart factory. This technological evolution ushers in the *Industry 4.0* as a prime agenda of the High-Tech Strategy 2020 Action Plan taken by the government of Germany, the Industrial Internet from General Electric in the United States of America, and the Internet+ from China. A human-centered approach that puts humans in the loop of today's CPS is the *Society 5.0* initiative of the 5th Science and Technology Basic Plan taken by the government of Japan [2]. By functionally integrating human beings at the social, cognitive, and physical levels, CPS become so-called *cyber-physical-social systems (CPSS)* [3].

Members of CPSS may engage in a wide variety of cyber-physical-social behaviors. The human-centeredness of Society 5.0 was recently investigated in technically greater detail in Gladden [4]. Gladden [4] describes the goal of Society 5.0 as the ability to create equal opportunities for all and to provide an environment that helps unleash the full potential of each individual. To do so, Society 5.0 will leverage on emerging Information and Communications Technology (ICT) to its fullest such that social barriers to each individual's self-realization are removed. For illustration, Fig. 5.1 depicts the transition from past to future societies and their co-evolution with industry [4–6].

Similar to Industry 4.0, Society 5.0 aims at seamlessly fusing the digital and physical worlds by using social robots, ambient intelligence, advanced human-computer interfaces (HCI), embodied AI, and various flavors of extended reality (XR), among others (see also Fig. 5.1). However, Society 5.0 tries to counterbalance the commercial emphasis of Industry 4.0. Toward this

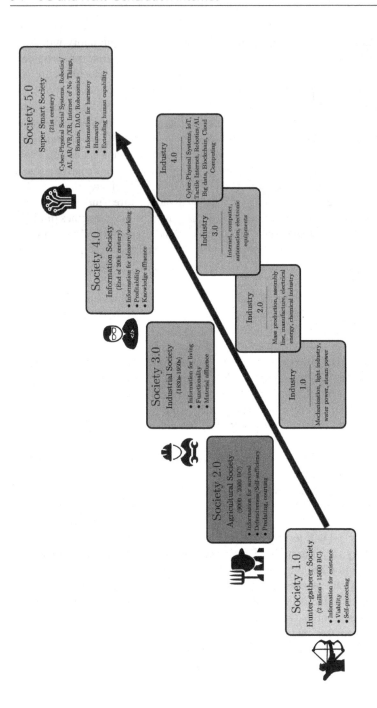

FIGURE 5.1 Co-evolution of Society and industry toward Society 5.0 [4, 5, 6].

end, the overarching goal of Society 5.0 will be the creation of the world's first super-smart society. Conversely, the focus of Industry 4.0 has been the creation of a smart factory that is fully automated and thus requires minimum human presence on-site. More interestingly, Society 5.0 also envisions a paradigm shift from conventional monetary to future nonmonetary economies based on technologies that can measure activities toward human cobecoming that have no monetary value (to be explained shortly in the context of *tokenomics*) [7].

It is interesting to note that the aforementioned Society 5.0 vision aligns surprisingly well with the far-reaching vision of future 6G networks. 6G is anticipated to be more human-centered than fifth generation (5G), which primarily focused on industry verticals such as smart grids or smart cities, as outlined in the world's first 6G white paper of the 6GFP. Maier [8] illustrated the potential of CPSS by presenting two prominent 5/6G examples of human-in-the-loop centric systems. The first one is the Tactile Internet, which is widely viewed as one of the most interesting 5G low-latency applications [9]. The second one is the future Internet of No Things, which serves as an important stepping stone toward ushering in the 6G post-smartphone era [10]. Arguably more important, we also elaborated on *robonomics*, an emerging field in the 6G era, and the role advanced blockchain technologies play in realizing the Society 5.0 vision.

In this chapter, we build on our recent work on robonomics in the 6G era. We aim at exploring advanced blockchain technologies that enable the next-generation Internet known as Web3, which leverages the concept of *tokenization* as a process for converting an item of value into digital tokens, thus giving rise to the aforementioned tokenomics. Tokenization digitally encapsulates assets as well as access rights and permissions to assets in the physical and digital world into units called tokens. We investigate the design of purpose-driven tokens to facilitate collaboration by incentivizing an autonomous group of people to individually contribute to Society 5.0. Toward this end, we first present our CPSS-based bottom-up multilayer token engineering framework, putting a particular focus on the key role of its incentive mechanism layer in the important problem of token design. We then explore the concept of *indirect communication* to maintain social cohesion by the coupling of social and environmental organization via traces in a stigmergy-enhanced Society 5.0, while steering its collective behavior toward the creation of tech-driven public goods.

The remainder of the chapter is structured as follows. "Society 5.0: From Robonomics to Tokenomics" section elaborates on the role of robonomics and tokenomics in Society 5.0. In "the Path (DAO) to a Human-Centered Society" section, we outline our proposed path to a human-centered society and explain purpose-driven tokens and token engineering in technically greater detail. Further, we introduce our CPSS-based bottom-up multilayer token engineering framework for a Society 5.0. In "From Superorganism to Stigmergic Society and Collective Intelligence in the 6G Era" section, we explain how our proposed framework can be applied to advance human collective intelligence in the 6G era. "Implementation and Experimental Results" section describes its experimental implementation and highlights some illustrative results. Finally, "Conclusions" section concludes the chapter.

SOCIETY 5.0: FROM ROBONOMICS TO TOKENOMICS

Cardenas and Kim [11] provided insights into how blockchain and other decentralized technologies have an impact on the interaction of humans with robot agents and their social integration into human society. Toward this end, blockchain technologies can serve as a ledger, where robots and humans may access and record anything of value, such as ownership titles or financial transactions. Further, smart contracts help encode the self-enforceable and self-verifiable agreement logic between a robot and a human. Cryptocurrencies may be used to allow robots to hold financial obligations and enter into exchanges of value with a human, and vice versa.

The shift from conventional monetary economics to nonmonetary tokenomics and the central role tokens play in blockchain-based ecosystems were analyzed recently by Freni et al. [12]. Decentralized blockchain technologies have been applied in a non-monetary context by exploiting a process known as *tokenization* in different value-based scenarios. The tokenization of an existing asset refers to the process of creating a *tokenized digital twin* for any physical object or financial asset. The resultant tokens are tradeable units that encapsulate value digitally. They can be used as incentives to coordinate actors in a given regulated ecosystem in order to achieve a desired outcome. According to Freni et al. [12], tokens have a disruptive potential to expand the concept of value beyond the economic realm by using them for reputation purposes or voting rights. Through tokenization, different types of digitized value can be exploited in an ecosystem of incentives by sharing the rewards and benefits among its stakeholders.

Tokens can represent any existing digital or physical asset, as well as access rights to assets and permissions in the digital or physical world. A token is stored as an entry in the ledger and is mapped to a blockchain address, which represents the identity of the token holder. Originally, tokens were minted by using the underlying blockchain protocols. However, with the advent of Ethereum, tokens moved up the blockchain protocol stack and can now be created on the application layer, giving rise to so-called application tokens. With Ethereum, application tokens can be issued easily and cheaply following the Ethereum token standards (e.g., ERC-20) via a specific type of smart contract, known as token contract.

Tokens might be the killer application of blockchain networks and are recognized as one of the main driving forces behind the next-generation Internet referred to as the Web3 [13]. As shown in Fig. 5.2, while the Web1 (read-only web) and Web2 (read-and-write web) enabled the knowledge economy and today's platform economy, respectively, the Web3 will enable the *token economy* where anyone's contribution is compensated with a token. The token economy enables completely new use cases, business models, and types of assets and access rights in a digital way that were economically not feasible before, thus enabling completely new use cases and value creation models. Note that the term token economy is far from novel. In cognitive psychology, it has been widely studied as a medium of exchange, and arguably more importantly, as a positive reinforcement method for establishing desirable human behavior, which in itself may be viewed as one kind of value creation. Unlike coins, however, which have been typically used only as a payment medium, tokens may serve a wide range of different non-monetary purposes. Such purpose-driven tokens are instrumental in incentivizing an autonomous group of individuals to collaborate and contribute to a common

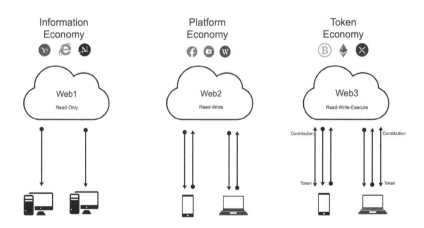

FIGURE 5.2 Evolution of Internet economy: From read-only Web1 information economy and read-write Web2 platform economy to read-write-execute Web3 token economy based on decentralized blockchain and self-executing smart contract technologies.

goal. According to Voshmgir [13], the exploration of tokens, in particular different types and roles, is still in the very early stages.

The token economy plays a central role in realizing the emerging decentralized autonomous organizations (DAO), which has become a hot topic spawned by the rapid development of blockchain technology in recent years [14]. The DAO may be viewed as a social system composed of intelligent agents coevolving into human-machine integration based on real-world and artificial blockchain systems. In the DAO, all the operational rules are recorded on the blockchain in the form of smart contracts. Token economy incentives together with distributed consensus protocols are utilized to realize the self-operation, self-governance, and self-evolution of the DAO. In fact, according to Wang et al. [14], the use of tokens as incentives is the main motivator for the DAO, whereby the so-called *incentive mechanism* layer of their presented multi-layer DAO reference model will be key for the token design (to be discussed in more detail shortly).

THE PATH (DAO) TO A HUMAN-CENTERED SOCIETY

While a lot of tokens have been issued over the last few years, most of these issued tokens lack proper functionality and mechanism design. In this section, we aim at addressing these two shortcomings by discussing purpose-driven tokens and introducing the important problem of token engineering.

Purpose-Driven Tokens and Token Engineering

Recall from "Society 5.0: From Robonomics to Tokenomics" section that we are still in the very early stages of exploring different roles and types of tokens. For instance, so-called *purpose-driven tokens* incentivize individual behavior to contribute to a certain purpose or idea of a collective goal. This collective goal might be a public good or the reduction of negative externalities to a common good, e.g., reduction of CO_2 emissions. Purpose-driven tokens introduce a new form of public goods creation without requiring traditional intermediaries, e.g., governments. Blockchain networks such as Ethereum took the idea of collective value creation to the next level by providing a public infrastructure for creating an application token with only a few lines of smart contract code, whereby in principle any purpose can be incentivized. However, given that operational use cases are still limited, this new phenomenon of tech-driven public goods creation needs much more research and development [13].

Proof-of-work (PoW) is an essential mechanism for the maintenance of public goods [13]. Even though the collective production of public goods can result in positive externalities, it does not necessarily exclude other negative externalities, e.g., energy-intense mining process of blockchains. When designing purpose-driven tokens as a means to provide public goods, behavioral economics methods, e.g., the well-known nudging technique and behavioral game theory, provide important tools to steer individuals toward certain actions.

In the following, we focus on the important problem of *token engineering*, which is an emerging term defined as the theory, practice, and tools to analyze, design, and verify tokenized ecosystems [13]. It involves the design of a bottom-up token engineering framework along with the design of adequate mechanisms for addressing the issues of purpose-driven tokens. Note that mechanism design is a subfield of economics that deals with the question of how to incentivize everyone to contribute to a collective goal. It is also referred to as "reverse game theory" since it starts at the end of the game (i.e., its desirable output) and then goes backward when designing the (incentive) mechanism.

Token Engineering DAO Framework for Society 5.0

Recall from "Society 5.0: From Robonomics to Tokenomics" section that for the token design a multilayer DAO reference model was proposed in [14], though it was intentionally kept generic without any specific relation to Society 5.0. The bottom-up architecture of the DAO reference model comprises the following five layers: (*i*) basic technology, (*ii*) governance operation, (*iii*) incentive mechanism, (*iv*) organization form, and (*v*) manifestation. Due to space constraints, we refer the interested reader to [14] for further information on the generic DAO reference model and a more detailed description of each layer. In the following, we adapt the generic DAO reference model to the specific requirements of Society 5.0 and highlight the modifications made in our CPSS-based bottom-up token engineering DAO framework.

Figure 5.3 depicts our proposed multilayer token engineering DAO framework for Society 5.0 that builds on top of state-of-the-art CPSS. While the Internet of Things as a prime CPS example has ushered in Industry 4.0, advanced CPSS such as the future Internet of No Things, briefly mentioned in the "Introduction," will be instrumental in ushering in Society 5.0. As explained in more detail in [10], the Internet of No Things creates a converged service platform for the fusion of digital and real worlds that offers

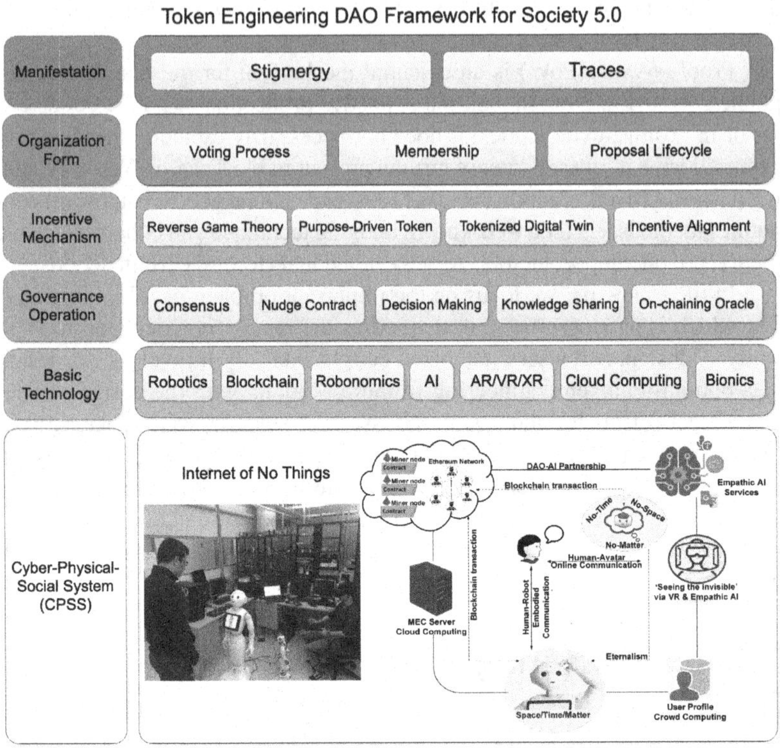

Token Engineering DAO Framework for Society 5.0

FIGURE 5.3 CPSS-based bottom-up token engineering DAO framework for Society 5.0.

all kinds of human-intended services without owning or carrying any type of computing or storage devices. It envisions Internet services appearing from the *surrounding environment* when needed and disappearing when not needed. The transition from the current gadgets-based Internet to the Internet of No Things is divided into three phases: (*i*) bearables (e.g., smartphone), (*ii*) wearables (e.g., Google and Levi's smart jacket), and then finally (*iii*) nearables. Nearables denote nearby computing/storage technologies and service provisioning mechanisms that are intelligent enough to *learn and react according to user context and history* in order to provide user-intended services. The basic technology layer at the bottom of Fig. 5.3 illustrates the key enabling technologies (e.g., blockchain) underlying the Internet of No Things. In addition, this layer contains future technologies, most notably bionics, that are anticipated to play an increasingly important role in a future super-smart Society 5.0 (see also Fig. 5.1).

Above the basic technology layer, there exists the governance operation layer. Generally speaking, this layer encodes consensus via smart contracts (e.g., voting) and realizes the DAO's self-governance through on-chain and off-chain collaboration (on-chaining oracle). Further, this layer includes nudging mechanisms via smart contract (nudge contract), collective decision-making, and knowledge sharing among its members. The incentive mechanism layer covers the aforementioned token-related techniques and their proper alignment to facilitate token engineering. Next, the organization form layer includes the voting process and membership during the lifecycle of a proposed DAO project. Note that, in economics, public goods that come with regulated access rights (e.g., membership) are called *club goods*.

Finally, the manifestation layer allows members to take simple, locally independent actions that together lead to the emergence of complex adaptive system behavior of the DAO and Society 5.0 as a whole. Due to its striking similarity to decentralized blockchain technology, we explore the potential of the biological *stigmergy* mechanism widely found in social insect societies such as ants and bees, especially their inherent capability of self-organization and indirect coordination by means of olfactory *traces* that members create in the environment. Upon sensing these traces, other society members are stimulated to perform succeeding actions, thus reinforcing the traces in a self-sustaining autocatalytic way without requiring any central control entity, as explained below in "From Superorganism to Stigmergic Society and Collective Intelligence in the 6G Era" section.

The Human Use of Human Beings: Cybernetics and Society

A prominent example of moving a Web2-based social network to Web3 was Facebook's recent announcement in June 2019 to launch a new infrastructure to manage their own token coined *Libra* (later renamed Diem), including suitable price stability mechanisms for its exchange with fiat currencies. However, the design of tokenized currencies will not be sufficient for realizing the Society 5.0 vision. To see this, note that people, including former and founding executives, began publicly questioning the impact of social media on our lives and opened up about their regrets over helping create social media as we know it today.[1] For instance, during a public discussion at the Stanford Graduate School of Business, Chamath Palihapitiya, former vice president of user growth at Facebook, told the Stanford audience that the tools we have created are ripping apart the social fabric of how society works. It is eroding the core foundation of how people behave by and between each other. He concluded that he doesn't have a good solution. His solution is just that he doesn't use these tools anymore, nor are his kids allowed to do so. Or, as Facebook's first president Sean Parker famously put it: "God only knows what it's doing to our children's brains."

Useful hints for more human-centered solutions may be found in the origins of cybernetics. In his seminal book "The Human Use of Human Beings: Cybernetics and Society," Norbert Wiener, the founder of cybernetics, argues that the danger of machines working on cybernetic principles, though helpless by themselves, is that such machines may be used by a human being or a block of human beings to increase their control over the rest of the human race. In order to avoid the manifold dangers of this, Wiener emphasizes the need for the anthropologist (see, e.g., [4]) and the philosopher. He postulates that scientists must know what man's nature is and what his built-in purposes are, arguing that the integrity of *internal communication* via feedback loops is essential to the welfare of society.

FROM SUPERORGANISM TO STIGMERGIC SOCIETY AND COLLECTIVE INTELLIGENCE IN THE 6G ERA

In this section, we explore how the aforementioned integrity of internal communication may be achieved in Society 5.0 by borrowing ideas from the biological superorganism with brain-like cognitive abilities observed in colonies of social insects. The concept of stigmergy (from the Greek words *stigma* "sign" and *ergon* "work"), originally introduced in 1959 by French zoologist Pierre-Paul Grassé, is a class of self-organization mechanisms that made it possible to provide an elegant explanation to his paradoxical observations that in a social insect colony, individuals work as if they were alone while their collective activities appear to be coordinated. In stigmergy, traces are left by individuals in their environment that may feed back on them and thus incite their subsequent actions. The colony records its activity in the environment using various forms of storage and uses this record to organize and constrain collective behavior through a feedback loop, thereby giving rise to the concept of *indirect communication*. As a result, stigmergy maintains social cohesion by coupling of environmental and social organization. Note that with respect to the evolution of social life, the route from solitary to social life might not be as complex as one may think. In fact, in the AI subfield of swarm intelligence, e.g., swarm robotics, stigmergy is widely recognized as one of the key concepts.

In the following, we illustrate how our CPSS-based token engineering DAO framework in Fig. 5.3 can be applied to Society 5.0 and describe the involved bottom-up design steps of suitable purpose-driven tokens and mechanisms:

- **Step1: Specify Purpose**

  Recall from "the Path (DAO) to a Human-Centered Society" section that the design of any tokenized ecosystem starts with a desirable output, i.e., its purpose. As discussed in the "Introduction," the goal of Society 5.0 is to provide a techno-social environment for CPSS members that (*i*) extends human capabilities and (*ii*) measures activities toward human co-becoming super smart. Toward this end, we advance AI to CI among swarms of connected human beings and things, as widely anticipated in the 6G era.

- **Step 2: Select CPSS of Choice**

  We choose our recently proposed Internet of No Things as state-of-the-art CPSS, since its final transition phase involves nearables that help create intelligent environments for providing human-centered and user-intended services (see "the Path (DAO) to a Human-Centered Society" section). Maier et al. [10] introduced an extrasensory perception network (ESPN), which integrates ubiquitous and persuasive computing in nearables (e.g., social robots, virtual avatars) to change the behavior of human users through social influence. In this chapter, we focus on blockchain and robonomics as the two basic technologies to expand *ESPN's online environment* and *offline agents*, respectively.

- **Step 3: Define PoW**

  Recall from "the Path (DAO) to a Human-Centered Society" section that PoW is an essential mechanism for the maintenance of tech-driven public goods. Specifically, we are interested in creating club goods, briefly mentioned in "the Path (DAO) to a Human-Centered Society" section, whose regulated access rights avoid the well-known "tragedy of the commons." [15] To regulate access, we exploit the advanced blockchain technology of *on-chaining oracles*. On-chaining oracles are instrumental in bringing external off-chain information onto the blockchain in a trustworthy manner. The on-chained information may originate from human users. Hence, on-chaining oracles help tap into human intelligence [16]. As PoW, we define the oracles' contributions to the governance operation of the CPSS via decision-making and knowledge sharing, which are both instrumental in achieving the specific purpose of CI.

- **Step 4: Design Tokens with Proper Incentive Alignment**
  Most tokens lack proper incentive mechanism design. Recall from "Society 5.0: From Robonomics to Tokenomics" section that the use of tokens as incentives lie at the heart of the DAO and their investigation has started only recently. Importantly, recall that the tokenization process creates *tokenized digital twins* to coordinate actors and regulate an ecosystem for the pursuit of a desired outcome by including *voting rights*. The creation of a tokenized digital twin is done via a *token contract* that incentivizes our defined PoW, involving the following two steps: (*i*) create digital twin that represents a given asset in the physical or digital world, and (*ii*) create one or more tokens that assign access rights/permissions of the given physical/digital asset to the blockchain address of the token holder.
- **Step 5: Facilitate Indirect Communication among DAO Members via Stigmergy & Traces**
  Finally, let the members participating in a given DAO project (*i*) record their purpose-driven token-incentivized activities in ESPN's blockchain-enabled online environment and (*ii*) use these blockchain transactions (e.g., deposits) as *traces* to steer the collective behavior toward higher levels of CI in a stigmergy enhanced Society 5.0.

Figure 5.4 illustrates the functionality of each of these five steps in more detail, including their operational interactions.

IMPLEMENTATION AND EXPERIMENTAL RESULTS

A general definition of human intelligence is the success rate of accomplishing tasks. In our implementation, human intelligence tasks (HIT) are realized by leveraging the image database ImageNet [2] widely used in deep learning research, and tokenizing it. Specifically, humans are supposed to discover a hidden reward map consisting of purpose-driven tokens by means of image tagging, which is done by relying on the crowd intelligence of Amazon Mechanical Turk (MTurk) workers and the validation of their answers via a voting-based decision-making blockchain oracle. We measure CI as the ratio of discovered/rewarded number and the total number of purpose-driven tokens.

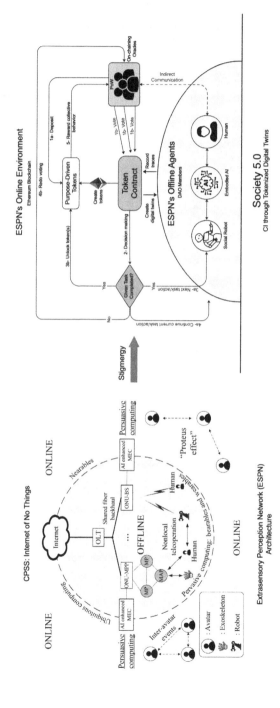

FIGURE 5.4   Stigmergy enhanced Society 5.0 using tokenized digital twins for advancing collective intelligence (CI) in CPSS.

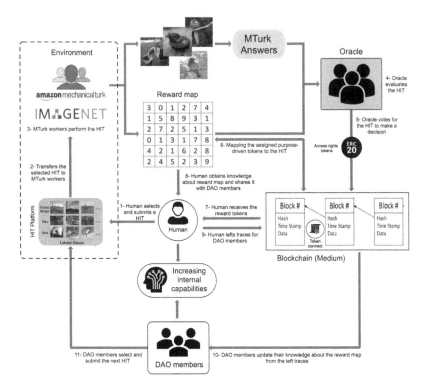

FIGURE 5.5 Discovery of hidden token reward map through individual or collective ImageNet tagging via Amazon MTurk and on-chaining Oracle.

Figure 5.5 depicts the set-up and experimental steps of our implementation in more detail. We developed a JavaScript-based HIT platform to let a human select from 20 ImageNet images as well as add relevant image tagging information and deliver both to the properly configured MTurk and Amazon Web Services (AWS) accounts using an intermediate OOCSI server. The answers provided by MTurk workers to each submitted HIT were evaluated by an on-chaining oracle, which used ERC-20 compliant access right tokens to regulate the voting process and release the purpose-driven tokens assigned to each successfully tagged image. Finally, the human leaves the discovered/ rewarded tokens as stigmergic traces on the blockchain to help participating DAO members update their knowledge about the reward map and continue its exploration.

Figure 5.6 shows the beneficial impact of stigmergy on both collective intelligence and internal reward in terms of hidden tokens discovered in the reward map by a DAO with eight members. For comparison, the figure also

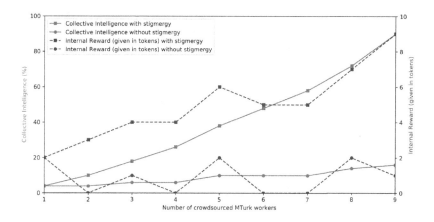

FIGURE 5.6   Collective intelligence (given in percent) and internal reward (given in tokens) with and without stigmergy vs. number of crowdsourced Amazon MTurk workers.

shows our experimental results without stigmergy, where the DAO members don't benefit from sharing knowledge about the unfolding reward map discovery process.

CONCLUSIONS

Society 5.0 nicely aligns with future 6G's anticipated shift from industry verticals to more human-centeredness. It leverages on CPSS that engage humans in cyber-physical-social behaviors and on technologies that enable a paradigm shift from conventional monetary to future non-monetary economies, such as our considered blockchain-based Web3 token economy and its important role in the recently emerging DAO. Given its similarity to decentralized blockchain technology, we adopted stigmergy—a biological self-organization mechanism widely found in social insect societies—for facilitating indirect communication and internal coordination among offline agents via traces (feedback loops) created in a blockchain-based online environment. Our implemented CPSS-based bottom-up token-engineering DAO framework for Society 5.0 was experimentally shown to increase both CI and rewarded purpose-driven tokens by means of stigmergic traces in a blockchain-based online environment involving crowdsourced Amazon MTurk workers and validating on-chaining oracle.

NOTES

1. https://gizmodo.com/former-facebook-exec-you-don-t-realize-it-but-you-are-1821181133
2. https://www.image-net.org

REFERENCES

1. K. B. Letaief; W. Chen; Y. Shi; J. Zhang and Y. A. Zhang, "The Roadmap to 6G: AI Empowered Wireless Networks," *IEEE Communications Magazine*, vol. 57, no. 8, pp. 84–90, Aug. 2019.
2. Government of Japan, "The 5th Science and Technology Basic Plan (Tentative Translation)," Dec. 2015. Available online: https://www8.cao.go.jp/cstp/kihonkeikaku/5basicplan_ en.pdf [accessed on Sep. 06, 2021].
3. Y. Zhou; F. R. Yu; J. Chen and Y. Kuo, "Cyber-Physical-Social Systems: A State-of-the-Art Survey, Challenges and Opportunities," *IEEE Communications Surveys & Tutorials*, vol. 22, no. 1, pp. 389–425, First Quarter 2020.
4. M. E. Gladden, "Who Will Be the Members of Society 5.0? Towards an Anthropology of Technologically Posthumanized Future Societies," *Social Sciences*, vol. 8, no. 5:148, pp.1–39, May 2019.
5. N. Berberich; T. Nishida and S. Suzuki, "Harmonizing Artificial Intelligence for Social Good," *Philosophy & Technolgy*, vol. 33, pp. 613–638, Dec. 2020.
6. M. Lammers, "Society 5.0: Discover how PropTech and the Sustainable Development Goals come together," *PropTechNL*, Oct. 2020. Available online: https://shorturl.at/irA13 [accessed on Sep. 06, 2021].
7. Hitachi-UTokyo Laboratory (H-UTokyo Lab), "Society 5.0: A People-Centric Super-Smart Society," *Springer Open*, Singapore, 2020.
8. M. Maier, "6G as if People Mattered: From Industry 4.0 toward Society 5.0 (Invited Paper)," *Proceedings of 30th International Conference on Computer Communications and Networks (ICCCN)*, pp. 1–10, Athens, Greece, July 2021.
9. M. Maier and A. Ebrahimzadeh, "Towards Immersive Tactile Internet Experiences: Low-Latency FiWi Enhanced Mobile Networks with Edge Intelligence [Invited]," *IEEE/OSA Journal of Optical Communications and Networking, Special Issue on Latency in Edge Optical Networks*, vol. 11, no. 4, pp. B10–B25, Apr. 2019.
10. M. Maier; A. Ebrahimzadeh; S. Rostami and A. Beniiche, "The Internet of No Things: Making the Internet Disappear and 'See the Invisible'," *IEEE Communications Magazine*, vol. 58, no. 11, pp. 76–82, Nov. 2020.
11. I. S. Cardenas; & J. H Kim, "Robonomics: The Study of Robot-Human Peer-to-Peer Financial Transactions and Agreements," *Proceedings of HRI '20: Companion of the 2020 ACM/IEEE International Conference on Human-Robot Interaction*, pp. 8–15, Cambridge, UK, March 2020.

12. P. Freni; E. Ferro and R. Moncada, "Tokenization and Blockchain Tokens Classification: A morphological framework," *Proceedings of EEE Symposium on Computers and Communications (ISCC)*, Rennes, France, pp. 1–6, July 2020.

13. S. Voshmgir, "Token Economy: How the Web3 reinvents the Internet (Second Edition)," *BlockchainHub*, Berlin, Germany, June 2020.

14. S. Wang; W. Ding; J. Li; Y. Yuan; L. Ouyang and F. Y. Wang, "Decentralized Autonomous Organizations: Concept, Model, and Applications," *IEEE Transactions on Computational Social Systems*, vol. 6, no. 5, pp. 870–878, Oct. 2019.

15. G. Hardin, "The Tragedy of the Commons: The population problem has no technical solution; it requires a fundamental extension in morality," *Science*, vol. 162, no. 3859, pp.1243–1248, 1968.

16. A. Beniiche; S. Rostami and M. Maier, "Robonomics in the 6G Era: Playing the Trust Game With On-Chaining Oracles and Persuasive Robots," *IEEE Access*, vol. 9, pp. 46949–46959, March 2021.

Conclusions

SUMMARY

The blockchain revolution is about to flip the status quo of centralized systems in most industries in favor of more decentralized, transparent, open, secure, and efficient infrastructures. While most people view blockchain from a transactional perspective, there are still many salient aspects of a true blockchain that people have not paid particular attention to. These facets, however, are responsible for the nature of the technology as we know it and the reason why it's set to revolutionize the way people transact with others in the near and distant future. Blockchain is changing our society on a fundamental level. It is transforming what we can do online, how we do it, and who can participate. This book examined the design and investigation of the pillars of human-centered blockchain technologies for the sixth generation (6G) era.

This book is based on blockchain as promising underlying human-centered technologies on which the 6G era is envisioned to rely. In particular, we studied different aspects of the emerging Tactile Internet and presented in-depth technical insights into realizing human-in-the-loop (HITL)-centric teleoperation Tactile Internet over FiWi-enhanced networks, including the synergies between the Human-Agent-Robot Teamwork (HART) membership and the complementary strengths of robots to facilitate local human-machine coactivity clusters by decentralizing the Tactile Internet using advanced blockchain technologies. Specifically, we studied the role of the Ethereum decentralized autonomous organizations (DAO) and human crowdsourcing in helping decrease task completion time in the event of unreliable connectivity and/or network failures. Further, we investigated the role of behavioral economics games in studying trust and trustworthiness between agents. From the outcome of our investigation and experimentation, we showed that our considered trust game of behavioral economics can be enhanced using basic and advanced Ethereum blockchain techniques and using persuasive robots strategies borrowed from the field of robonomics. Finally, the book explored

DOI: 10.1201/9781003427322-6

Society 5.0 as an important stepping stone toward realizing the vision of human-centered 6G mobile networks. Our focus was on exploring the role of the DAO, CPSS, and the future Web3 and its underlying token economy toward realizing collective intelligence in a stigmergic society. In the following, a more detailed summary of each chapter is presented.

In Chapter 2, we showed that many of the emerging blockchain Internet of Things (B-IoT) studies use Ethereum as the blockchain of choice and apply a gateway-oriented design approach to offload computationally intensive tasks from resource-constrained end-devices onto an intermediate gateway, thus enabling them to access the Ethereum blockchain network. Toward this end, we first explained the commonalities of and specific differences between Ethereum and Bitcoin blockchains followed by a description of the DAO in technically greater detail. We then discussed the motivation for the integration of blockchain and IoT (B-IoT) followed by a description of the challenges of integrating blockchain and edge computing. Building on our recent Tactile Internet work on orchestrating hybrid HART coactivities, we introduced our proposed low-latency FiWi enhanced LTE-A HetNets based on advanced MEC with embedded AI capabilities. We then showed that higher levels of decentralized AI-enhanced MEC are effective in reducing the average completion time of computational tasks. Further, for remote execution of physical tasks in a decentralized Tactile Internet, we explored how Ethereum's DAO and smart contracts may be used to establish trusted HART membership and how human crowdsourcing helps decrease physical task completion time in the event of unreliable forecasting of haptic feedback samples from teleoperated robots. We outlined future research avenues on technological convergence in order to successfully accomplish hybrid machine+human tasks by augmented and shared intelligence tapping into the theory of nudge, a recent novel development in behavioral economics concept popularized by Richard H. Thaler, the 2017 Nobel Laureate in Economics.

In Chapter 3, we explored how Ethereum blockchain technologies, in particular the aforementioned concept of the DAO, may be leveraged to decentralize the Tactile Internet, which enables unprecedented mobile applications for remotely steering real or virtual objects/processes in perceived real-time and represents a promising example of future techno-social systems. We showed that a higher level of decentralization of AI-enhanced MEC reduces the average computational task completion time of up to 89.5% by setting the computation offloading probability to 0.7. Further, we observed that crowdsourcing of human assistance is beneficial in decreasing the average completion time of physical tasks for medium to high feedback misforecasting probabilities, provided the human offers equal or even superior operational capabilities, i.e., $\frac{f_{human}}{f_{robot}} \geq 1$. Toward this end, we proposed a nudge contract as a technique to influence nearby human behavior without punishment for skills transfer in the context of the Tactile Internet. Specifically, the nudge contract aims to enable the skills transfer process as well as a reward by means of the Ethereum smart contract. We then showed that the considered nudge contract helps successfully accomplish tasks via shared intelligence among failing robots and skilled humans.

In Chapter 4, we covered some of the ways in which our decisions are affected by social influences and the behavior and attitude of other people. Toward this end, we investigated the widely studied trust game of behavioral economics in a blockchain context. Besides the design of a decentralized trust game without the need for the experimenter in the middle between players, we presented a simple but efficient blockchain-based mechanism of deposit as a pre-commitment between players. The term pre-commitment was first introduced in 1978 by Thomas Schelling, the 2005 Nobel Laureate in Economics as part of a self-management system called *Egonomics*[1]. Later in 1979, the Norwegian philosopher, social, and political theorist Jon Elster developed the theory of pre-commitment, which he also calls self-binding in his work *Ulysses and the Sirens*[2]. Using this mechanism, we experimentally demonstrated that a social efficiency of up to 100% can be achieved to enhance both trust and trustworthiness between players (and thus investment and reciprocity). Further, we presented a voting-based on-chaining blockchain oracle architecture for a networked N-player trust game that involves a third type of player called observers, whose primary goal is to observe, track, and reward/punish players' behavior depending on their investment and reciprocity. The resultant peer pressure by the on-chaining oracle helps raise average normalized reciprocity above 80%. Finally, we experimentally demonstrated that players are more likely to give more when their generosity is made public and encouraged by social robots, especially by leveraging the mixed logical-affective persuasive strategies for social robots of the emerging field of robonomics.

In Chapter 5, we explained that 6G will differ from fifth generation (5G) in several ways. 6G will not only explore more spectrum at high-frequency bands but also converge driving technological trends, including connected robotics and blockchain technologies. Importantly, we showed that 6G will become more human-centered than 5G, which primarily focused on industry verticals. Putting people at the center of a future super-smart society is the driving theme for the anticipated shift of research focus from Industry 4.0 to Society 5.0 based on CPSS, which integrates human beings at the social, cognitive, and physical levels and engages them in cyber-physical-social behaviors with diverse types of meta-human capabilities. Specifically, we focus on the paradigm shift from conventional monetary to future non-monetary economies, such as our considered blockchain-based Web3 token economy and its important role in the recently emerging DAO. Toward this end, we presented our CPSS-based token engineering DAO framework for Society 5.0. Given its similarity to decentralized blockchain technology, we adopted stigmergy—a biological self-organization mechanism widely found in social insect societies—for facilitating indirect communication and internal coordination among offline agents via traces (feedback loops) created in a blockchain-based online environment. Most notably, we studied indirect communication mediated by tokenized digital twins to advance collective intelligence in a future Society 5.0 and a token economy-based Web3, where humans act like neurons in a hive mind with blockchain technology acting as connecting tissue to create programmable incentives known as tokens. Finally, we experimentally showed how to increase both Collective Intelligence (CI) and rewarded purpose-driven tokens by means of stigmergic traces in a blockchain-based online environment involving crowdsourced Amazon MTurk workers and validating on-chaining oracle.

NOTES

1. T. C. Schelling, "Egonomics, or the Art of Self-Management," *The American Economic Review*, May 1978.
2. Jon Elster, "Ulysses and the Sirens: Studies in Rationality and Irrationality," *Cambridge University Press*, 1979.

Index

Page numbers in **bold** refer to tables and those in *italic* refer to figures.

A

Access control contracts (ACCs), 55
ACP approach, 18
Advanced persistent threat (APT), 36
Affective strategy, 86
AI-enhanced MEC servers, *43*, 43–44,
 58–60, *60*
Altruistic punishment, 74
ALVideoDevice, Django server, 85
Amazon Mechanical Turk (MTurk), 104, *106*
Amazon Web Services (AWS), 106
Ambient intelligence, 93
Application Binary Interface (ABI), 75
Application programming interface (API),
 30–31
Application tokens, 97
Aragon platform, 12
Artificial general intelligence (AGI), 63
Artificial neural network (ANN), 61
Augmented/virtual reality (AR/VR), 2

B

Base stations (BSs), 5
Bearables, 100
BeCome, edge computing capabilities, 37
Blockchain 1.0, 8
Blockchain-enabled edge computing, 36–38
Blockchain Internet of Things (B-IoT), 27,
 33–36, 111
 ACCs, 55
 decentralized ownership, 55
 problems, 55
Blockchain mechanism deposit
 e-Deliveries service, 76
 experimental setup, 77
 Function deposit() function, 76
 Function splitFraction() function, 76
Blockchain oracles
 centralized or decentralized, 13
 Chainlink, 14

challenges, 15
classification, 13
combinations, 13
design patterns, 13–14
 Orisi, 14
 Reality Keys, 14
software, hardware and human, 13
Town Crier, 14–15
validation oracles, 14
Blockchain technology; *see also* Blockchain
 oracles; Ethereum *vs* bitcoin
 blockchains
DApps, 8–9
decentralized, 25, 26
emergence of Bitcoin, 8
ethereum, 8, 26
evolution of, 9, *10*
financial and non-financial applications, 8
next-generation platforms, 9
oracle problem, 10
transaction workflow, 8, *9*
"BlockTDM," data management scheme, 37

C

Centralized oracles, 13
Chainlink, 14
Clear To Send (CTS), 59
Cognitive-assistance-based intelligence
 amplification, 48, 62–63
Cognitive augmentation, 48
Collective intelligence (CI), 92, *107*, 113
Colony platform, 12–3
Computation-oriented communications
 (CoC), 58
Coordinated multipoint (CoMP) transmission
 and reception, 1–2
CPSS-based bottom-up token engineering
 DAO framework, *100*
Crowd-of-Oz (CoZ) platform, 84
Crowdsourcing, 47, *47*, 60–62, *62*
Cryptocurrencies, 96

Cryptocurrency smart card (CCSC), 34–35
Cybernetics and society, 101–102
Cyber-physical-social systems (CPSS), 16–17, 93
Cyber-physical systems (CPS), 93

D

DAOstack platform, 12
Data feeds, 10
Decentralized applications (DApps), 8–9, 30–31
Decentralized autonomous organization (DAO), 9–10, 26, 31–33, *32*, **33**, *98*, 110
  Aragon, 12
  Colony, 12–3
  DAOstack, 12
  decision-making process, 11
  MakerDAO, 11
  online governance, 11
Decentralized edge intelligence, 45–46, *46*
Decentralized oracles, 13
Decentralized self-organizing cooperative (DSOC) concept, 49, 63–64
Digital video broadcasting (DVB), 1
Distributed Coordination Function Interframe Space (DIFS), 59
Distributed ledger technology (DLT), 7–8, 26, 70; *see also* Blockchain technology
DNSLedger, 36
Domain name system (DNS), 36

E

Edge computing, 36
Edge sample forecasting (ESF) module, 58
Electronic Delivery (e-Deliveries) service, 76
Elliptic curve digital signature algorithm (ECDSA), 35
Enhanced mobile broadband (Embb), 2
ERC-20 Standard token, 15–16
ERC-721 Standard token, 16
ERC-1155 Standard token, 16
Ether, 30
Ethereum Externally Owned Account (EOA), 75
Ethereum, open software platform, 8, 54
Ethereum virtual machine (EVM), 8, 30
Ethereum *vs.* bitcoin blockchains
  commonalities and differences, 28, *29*
  ledger, 28

programming languages, 30
  public *vs.* private blockchains, 28, *28*
  types of actors, roles of, 29
EVM byte code, 75
Evolution of internet economy, *97*
Experimenter smart contract, 75–76
Extrasensory perception (ESP), 4
Extrasensory perception network (ESPN), 4, *5*

F

Fifth generation (5G) networks, 55
Firewalls, 31
First generation (1G) mobile network, 1
FiWi access networks, 41, 110
  AI-enhanced agents, 57
  architecture of, 56, *57*
  CoC, 58
  EPON fiber backhaul, 57
Fourth generation (4G) mobile network, 1
Function deposit() function, 76
Function investFraction() function, 75
Function splitFraction() function, 75, 76

G

6Genesis Flagship Program (6GFP), 72
Global system for mobile (GSM) communication, 1

H

Hardware oracles, 13
Heterogeneous networks (HetNets), 41
  AI-enhanced MEC server, *43*, 43–44
  low-latency FiWi-enhanced LTE-A, 41–43, *42*
High-Tech Strategy 2020 Action Plan, 93
HITL hybrid-augmented intelligence, 48–49, 63
Human-agent-robot teamwork (HART), 27, 40–41
Human-Agent-Robot Teamwork (HART) membership, 110
Human augmentation, 49–50
Human-computer interfaces (HCI), 19, 93
Human crowdsourcing, 110
Human intelligence tasks (HIT), 104
Human-in-the-loop (HITL), 3, 56, 110
Human operators (HOs), 5, 44
Human oracles, 13

Humans-are-better-at/machines-are-better-at (HABA/MABA) approach, 41
Human-system interface (HSI), 58
Human-to-machine (H2M) interaction, 56
Human-to-machine/robot (H2M/R) interaction, 3

I

Industry 4.0, 93–94, *94*
Industry 5.0, 17–18
Information and Communications Technology (ICT), 93
Initial Coin Offering (ICO), 11
Intelligence amplification (IA)
  cognitive-assistance-based intelligence amplification, 48
  definition, 48
  DSOC, 49
  HITL hybrid-augmented intelligence, 48–49
  human augmentation, 49–50
Intelligent resource management, 71
Interactive systems, 2–3
International Mobile Telecommunications 2020 (IMT 2020) standard, 2
Internet of Everything (IoE), 71
Internet of No Things, 4, 95, 100
Internet of things (IoT), 2, 54, 93
Internet Protocol (IP) based network, 1
Inter-Planetary File System (IPFS), 64
ITU-T Technology Watch Report, *3*

J

Judge contract (JC), 55

K

Key performance indicators (KPIs), 7
k-out-of-M threshold signature scheme, 81

L

Logical strategy, 86
Long-range (LoRa) wireless radio frequency, 35
Low-power wide-area (LPWA) technologies, 35
LTE-advanced (LTE-A) technique, 1–2, 41

M

Machine-augmented intelligence, 48
Machine-to-machine (M2M) communication, 3, 27, 34, 56
MakerDAO, 11
Management hub, 34
Many-worlds interpretation (MWI), 18
Massive machine-type communications (mMTC), 2, 26, 70
Miners, 29
Mixed strategy, 86
Mobile networks and internet, evolution of;
    see also Sixth generation (6G) mobile networks
  generations, coverage of, 1
  5G low-latency applications, 2
  3GPP, 1
  interactive systems, 2–3
  2 Mbit/s and enabled advanced services, 1
  revolutionary leap, Tactile Internet, *3*
  techniques, 1–2
Multi-access edge computing (MEC), 36–37
Multiple-input multiple-output (MIMO), 1–2

N

Nearables, 100
Network address translation (NAT), 31
Networked N-player trust game, 73–74
  on-chaining, voting-based decisions, 81
  oracle, architecture of, 79, *80*, 81
Non-fungible tokens (NFT), 16
Nudge
  contract, 65–66
  defined, 64
  functions, 81
  learning loss (in seconds) *vs.* subtask learning probability, 64, *65*
  remote decentralized storage server, 64

O

Offer network of mutual dependency, 49, 64
Optical line terminal (OLT), 5, 44
Optical network units (ONUs), 5, 44
Oracle problem, 10
Oracles, 68
Orthogonal frequency division multiplexing (OFDM), 1–2

P

Parameter Onlytrustee (modifier type)
    modifier, 75
Parameter Onlytrustor (modifier type)
    modifier, 76
Peer-to-peer (P2P) platform, 25
Persuasive computing, 4, *5*
Persuasive robotics strategies
    CoZ user interface, 84
    IFrame HTML element, 85
    LED colors, 85
    logical and affective strategy, 86
    mixed strategy, 86
    OOCSI middleware, 85
    social cue buttons, 85–86, **87**
    speech-to-text function, 84–85
Pervasive computing, 4, *5*
Physical Layer (PHY), 59
Proof-of-stake (PoS) consensus, 30
Proof-of-work (PoW), 99
Proteus effect, 4
Provable Things, 14
Pull-based inbound oracle, 13
Pull-based outbound oracle, 13
Purpose-driven tokens, 98–99
Push-based inbound oracle, 13
Push-based outbound oracle, 13

R

Radio Access Network (RAN), 36–37
Reality Keys, 14
Regular nodes, 29
Remote APDU call secure (RACS), 35
Reward & penalty mechanism design, 74
Robonomics
    average normalized reciprocity, *88*
    experimental setup, 86–88
    persuasive robotics strategies, 84–86
    principles, 83–84

S

Second generation (2G) mobile network, 1
Self-sovereign identity (SSI) paradigm, 71
Service level agreement (SLA) management,
    71
Short Interframe Space (SIFS), 59
Short message service (SMS), 1
SingularityNET, 63

Sixth generation (6G) mobile network
    blockchain benefits, 70–71
    blockchains and robots, 71–72
    cloud service, 6
    grant-free transmissions, 6
    higher frequencies with wider system
        bandwidth, 6
    intelligent resource management, 71
    KPIs, 7
    massive MIMO, 6
    mMTC, 6–7
    security and privacy features, 71
    smartphones, 7–8
    transmission network, 7
    trustworthy 6G communications, 71
    wireless summit, 7
Smart contracts, 30, 54
Social efficiency, 72–73
    vs. deposit, *82*
    and normalized reciprocity, 77–79, *78*
Social human-robot interaction (sHRI), 84
Social robots, 93
Social singularity, 93
Society 5.0, 18–19, 93–94, *94*, 96–98, *97*,
    99–101, *100*, 111
Software oracles, 13
Stigmergy concept
    class of self-organization mechanisms,
        102
    design tokens, proper incentive alignment,
        104
    hidden token reward map, *106*
    indirect communication, 102, 104
    PoW, defined, 103
    select CPSS of choice, 103
    specify purpose, 103
    tokenized digital twins, *105*
Storj, automated smart contract
    operation, 31

T

The Tactile Internet
    defined, 2
    HART, 40–41, 45
    H2M/R interaction, 3
    principles, 38–40, *39*
    revolutionary leap, *3*
Technological singularity, 93
Teleoperator robot (TOR), 3, 5, 44
Third generation (3G) mobile network, 1

Token engineering, 15–16
  purpose-driven tokens, 98–99
  Society 5.0, 99–101, *100*
Tokenization, 96
Trust game, decentralized blockchain
    technologies
  economic experiments, 74–75
  N-Player Trust Game, 73–74
  reward & penalty mechanism
    design, 74
  social efficiency, 72–73
Trustor and trustee, 69, *69*

U

Ubiquitous computing, 4, *5*
Ultra-reliable and low-latency
    communication (URLLC), 2, 25,
    56, 70
Uniform Resource Locator (URL), 85

V

Vanity-ETH generators, 81
Virtual Private Network (VPN), 85
Voting-based games, 68

W

Wearables, 100
WiFi offloading ratio (WOR) values, 42, *42*
Wireless-optical broadband access networks
    (WOBANs), 41
Witnet, 14
Wizard-of-Oz (WoZ) manner, 84
WLAN mesh portal points (MPPs), 5

Z

Zurich Toolbox for Ready-made Economics
    (z-Tree), 74–75

Printed in the United States
by Baker & Taylor Publisher Services